T0283210

# A Methodology for Quantifying the Value of Cybersecurity Investments in the Navy

BRADLEY WILSON, MARK V. ARENA, LAUREN A. MAYER,
CHAD HEITZENRATER, JASON MASTBAUM, KEVIN J. CONNOLLY

Prepared for the United States Navy
Approved for public release; distribution unlimited

NATIONAL DEFENSE RESEARCH INSTITUTE

For more information on this publication, visit **www.rand.org/t/RRA1356-1**.

## About RAND

The RAND Corporation is a research organization that develops solutions to public policy challenges to help make communities throughout the world safer and more secure, healthier and more prosperous. RAND is nonprofit, nonpartisan, and committed to the public interest. To learn more about RAND, visit www.rand.org.

## Research Integrity

Our mission to help improve policy and decisionmaking through research and analysis is enabled through our core values of quality and objectivity and our unwavering commitment to the highest level of integrity and ethical behavior. To help ensure our research and analysis are rigorous, objective, and nonpartisan, we subject our research publications to a robust and exacting quality-assurance process; avoid both the appearance and reality of financial and other conflicts of interest through staff training, project screening, and a policy of mandatory disclosure; and pursue transparency in our research engagements through our commitment to the open publication of our research findings and recommendations, disclosure of the source of funding of published research, and policies to ensure intellectual independence. For more information, visit www.rand.org/about/principles.

RAND's publications do not necessarily reflect the opinions of its research clients and sponsors.

Published by the RAND Corporation, Santa Monica, Calif.
© 2022 RAND Corporation
**RAND®** is a registered trademark.

Library of Congress Control Number: 2022917271
ISBN: 978-1-9774-1002-3

*Cover: U.S. Navy photo by Petty Officer 2nd Class Lewis Hunsaker.*

# About This Report

The Office of the Chief of Naval Operations for Information Warfare (OPNAV N2/N6) asked the RAND Corporation to develop and support the implementation of a methodology to assess the value of resource options for U.S. Navy cybersecurity investments.

The proposed methodology draws from a variety of resources and enables OPNAV N2/N6 to rationalize the cost-effectiveness of potential Navy cybersecurity investments without the added complexity of monetizing potential losses from cybersecurity attacks or considering the probability of such events amid all possible adversaries and attack paths.

The methodology features 12 scales in two categories (impact and exploitability) that allow OPNAV N2/N6 to score potential investments. This report includes a test implementation using publicly available historical U.S. Navy data to demonstrate how the methodology facilitates valuable comparisons of potential cybersecurity investments.

## RAND National Security Research Division

This research was sponsored by the U.S. Navy Office of the Chief of Naval Operations (OPNAV) and conducted within the Navy and Marine Forces Center of the RAND National Security Research Division (NSRD), which operates the National Defense Research Institute (NDRI), a federally funded research and development center sponsored by the Office of the Secretary of Defense, the Joint Staff, the Unified Combatant Commands, the Navy, the Marine Corps, the defense agencies, and the defense intelligence enterprise.

For more information on the RAND Navy and Marine Forces Center, see www.rand.org/nsrd/nmf or contact the director (contact information is provided on the webpage).

## Acknowledgments

We thank Mr. Heath Bjordahl and CDR Durke Wright from OPNAV N2N6D5 for their guidance and insights during the methodology development.

Finally, Paul DeLuca and Brendan Toland, director and associate director, respectively, of the Navy and Marine Forces Center, provided valuable guidance and insightful comments on this research.

# Summary

The Office of the Chief of Naval Operations for Information Warfare (OPNAV N2/N6) asked the RAND Corporation to develop and support the implementation of a methodology to assess the value of resource options for U.S. Navy cybersecurity investments.

## Motivation

The objective of this research was to provide decisionmakers and analysts with an alternative method to explore prioritization options and assess alternatives during the Planning, Programming, Budgeting, and Execution process. OPNAV N2/N6 staff viewed current approaches as useful but limited, particularly because they do not help the office assess the cost-effectiveness of potential cybersecurity investments relative to one another. An important constraint in developing the methodology was that it needed to be practical for OPNAV N2/N6 to implement amid the following challenges, among others:

- Upstream decisionmaking filters the potential set of investments before they reach OPNAV N2/N6.
- There is limited information on investments.
- Data capture broad classes and types of investments.
- It is difficult to compare past- and future-year investments.
- Analysts and decisionmakers must choose from a broad set of potential investment prioritization strategies.
- There are challenges in quantifying the impact of an investment.

## Approach

We conducted an extensive literature review, interviewed subject-matter experts, and considered a myriad of possible approaches in developing the methodology. We examined the current OPNAV N2/N6 process, which includes the use of the Naval Information Warfare Systems Command–developed Force Level Integration Tool (FLINT). We reviewed a relevant Naval Air Systems Command approach, Cyber Risk Assessment (CRA), and Naval Sea Systems Command's Cyber Vulnerability Assessment Tool (CVAST). We also studied relevant federal information security guidance, such as the National Institute of Standards and Technology's (NIST's) Risk Management Framework and Cybersecurity Framework. We further reviewed information security economics literature and characterized the advantages and limitations of various economic metrics and models. Finally, we reviewed approaches to cybersecurity valuation metrics that were less economically oriented and more focused on defense missions.

We ultimately proposed a methodology that drew from many of these resources and that enable OPNAV N2/N6 to rationalize the cost-effectiveness of potential Navy cybersecurity investments, without the added complexity of having to monetize potential loss from cybersecurity attacks or consider the probability of specific events amid all possible adversaries and attack paths. Figure S.1 shows the scope of the proposed methodology.

We developed 12 scales in two categories (impact and exploitability) that enable OPNAV N2/N6 to score potential investments from 1 to 5, with 1 being low and 5 being high. Then we test-implemented the methodology using publicly available historical Navy budget estimating justification book data for fiscal years 2018 and 2020. In doing so, we were able to demonstrate how cybersecurity investments can be compared, as shown in Figure S.2.

## Key Findings

There is no silver bullet to the challenges of managing the highly complex tradespace of cyberattack risk (i.e., vulnerability), quantifying potential losses, and assessing the potential benefits of a particular cybersecurity investment. However, our methodology balances the needs of OPNAV N2/N6 with the available data and practical time and programmatic constraints. We did not model the approach after the NIST Cybersecurity Framework, but the scope of our methodology spans the scope of NIST's five categories: identify, protect, detect, respond, and recover.

**FIGURE S.1**

**Scope of the Proposed OPNAV N2/N6 Cybersecurity Valuation Methodology**

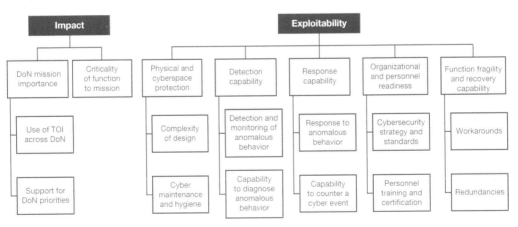

NOTE: DoN = U.S. Department of the Navy. TOI = target of investment.

FIGURE S.2

**Example Output from the Proposed Methodology**

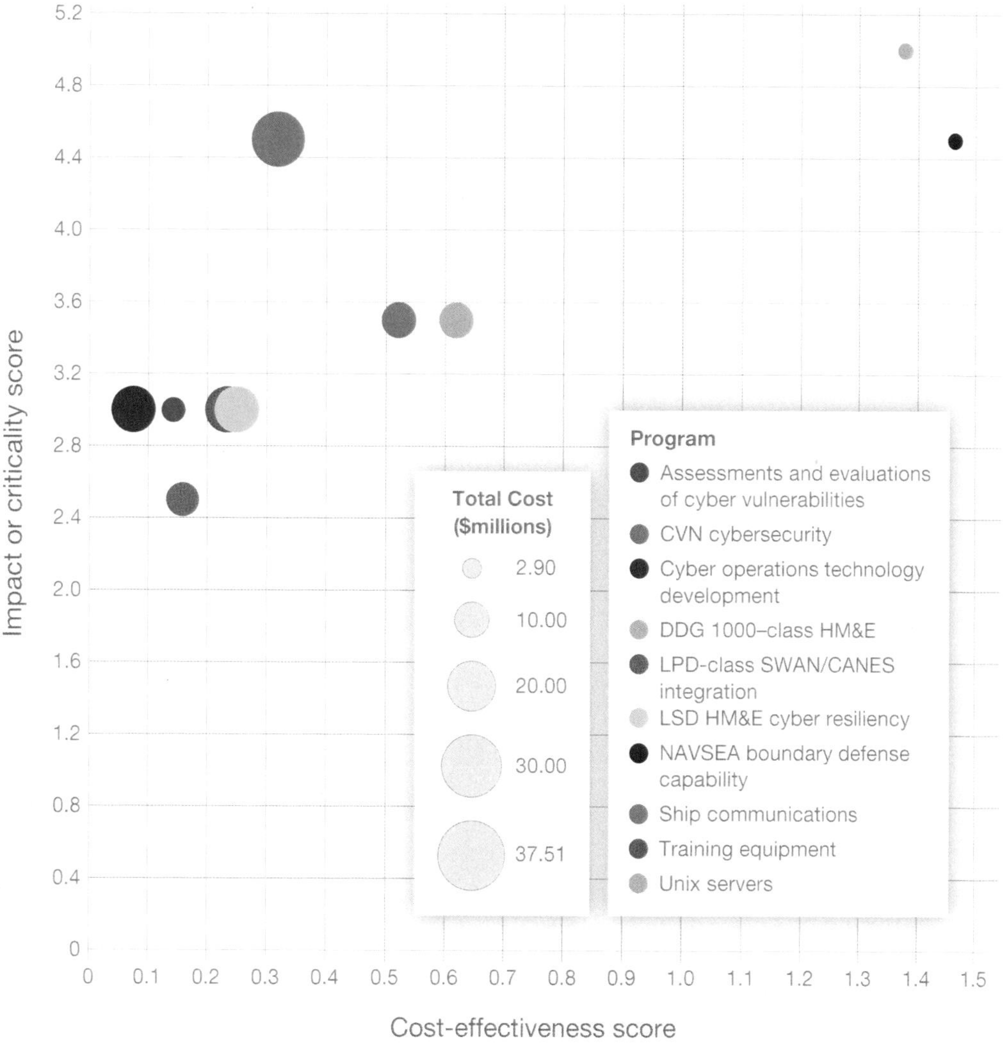

NOTE: CVN = nuclear aircraft carrier. DDG = guided missile destroyer. HM&E = hull, mechanical, and electrical. LPD = landing platform dock. NAVSEA = Naval Sea Systems Command.

# Recommendations

Next steps would include piloting this methodology and assessing its practical utility for OPNAV N2/N6 as part of its next program objective memorandum cycle. Chapter Two provides specific steps for implementation. The methodology—and, particularly, the proposed scales—could be improved through further iteration, including to develop a more structured approach to assessing investment data. Two additional recommendations arose in the course of this research:

1. **Provide a structured data framework for recommended investments, ideally through a web portal instead of PowerPoint slides.** This would, at a minimum, enable OPNAV N2/N6 to compare investments more quickly and also would mitigate the challenges of comparing past- and future-year investments. The existing FLINT portal could be adapted for this purpose.

2. **Within the data framework, provide common fields that represent Navy priorities and the scope of the investment.** In applying our impact scales, we found that it was challenging to rationalize between investments because we did not know the scope at which they operated (e.g., in terms of numbers of users supported, numbers of ships or aircraft supported or affected). It is critical for investment requests to include this information to increase understanding of a given investment's potential impact relative to that of others. Similarly, having structured, codified, and consistent priorities across investments also enables rapid comparative analysis.

# Contents

# Figures and Tables

## Figures

## Tables

# CHAPTER ONE

# Motivation, Challenges, and Relevant Literature

The Office of the Chief of Naval Operations for Information Warfare (OPNAV N2/N6) asked the RAND Corporation to develop and support the implementation of a methodology to assess the value of resource options for U.S. Navy cybersecurity investments.

## Motivation

As a resource sponsor, OPNAV N2/N6 must prioritize investments (or issues) that are required to address shortfalls of needs across the five-year Future Years Defense Program (FYDP) and outline the investment and required resources for inclusion in a yearly program objective memorandum (POM) (Blickstein et al., 2016, p. 10). A later step in the programming process prioritizes the OPNAV N2/N6 needs among those of the broader Navy.

The objective of the methodology is to provide decisionmakers and analysts with an alternative method to explore prioritization, options, and resource alternatives during the Planning, Programming, Budgeting, and Execution (PPBE) process. The current approach is viewed as useful but limited, particularly in terms of the cost-effectiveness of the potential investments relative to each other.

An important constraint is that any proposed methodology must be practical for OPNAV N2/N6 to implement. The methodology proposed in this study is intended to be applied during the programming phase of the PPBE process.

## Challenges

Making cybersecurity resource management choices during the PPBE process is challenging for OPNAV N2/N6 analysts and decisionmakers, even beyond the core challenge of operating in a resource-constrained environment. Some specific challenges are as follows:

- Upstream decisionmaking filters the potential set of investments before they reach the Office of the Chief for Naval Operations (OPNAV).
- There is limited information on investments.

- Data capture broad classes and types of investments.
- It is difficult to compare past- and future-year investments.
- Analysts and decisionmakers must choose from a broad set of potential investment prioritization strategies.
- There are challenges in quantifying the impact of an investment.[1]

Any proposed methodology would have to address these challenges in some way, and we discuss the implications in the following sections.

## Upstream Decisionmaking

OPNAV N2/N6 does not generate a list of potential investments to address shortfalls of need for the cybersecurity posture of the Navy on its own. It relies on such upstream organizations as Systems Commands, Fleet Forces Command, and Combatant Commands to help identify, assess, and prioritize investments within OPNAV N2/N6's capability portfolio. What makes this challenging is that the upstream planning processes (within PPBE) that shape the pool of potential investments are not necessarily transparent to OPNAV N2/N6.

## Limited Information on Investments

In many cases, the data that the OPNAV N2/N6 requests and receives from an upstream organization regarding an individual investment are in a single Microsoft PowerPoint slide outlining the needed investment. The slide typically displays the

- capability or program description
- rationale for adjustments
- warfighting capability impact of adjustment
- mission impact
- cybersecurity impact
- memorandum of agreement required
- contract termination liability
- prioritization
- focus area
- cyber resiliency improvement
- cost of the investment over the FYDP
- significant congressional or industrial impact.

The slide generally follows a template, but all fields are not necessarily completed. The slide also includes a great deal of free text, making it difficult to automatically export the

---

[1] These challenges are sourced from our interviews with Navy staff and from our first-hand observations of the data available to OPNAV N2/N6.

data. Too much information can bog down the programming process, but, as we discuss later in our review of methods for prioritizing cybersecurity, many of these methods require considerably more information than is available to OPNAV N2/N6 in the slides.

## Broad Classes and Types of Investments

The scope of investments under consideration spans the breadth of the U.S. Department of the Navy (DoN), from shipboard systems to back-office human resources and everything in between. The result is a set of investments that can be quite disparate in their scope and application, making comparison between investments challenging. Furthermore, the prefiltering that the upstream organizations do also can lead to aggregation of investments at different scales, which complicates comparative analysis.

## Challenges Comparing Past- and Future-Year Investments

Although OPNAV N2/N6 is considering the five-year FYDP period, "portions past the first year or two are less certain to reach the execution phase than they are to reach budget submission," necessitating adjustments by upstream organizations during each yearly POM cycle (Blickstein et al., 2016, p. 11). The adjustments to POM investment recommendations from year to year are not always evident to OPNAV N2/N6.

## A Broad Set of Potential Investment Prioritization Strategies

All the previous challenges involve the set of investments and scope provided to OPNAV N2/N6 to do its prioritization. However, there are also challenges involved in the analysis of the investments and their alignment to statutes, regulations, and other policy guidance, such as DoN priorities (e.g., DoN, 2021). As acquisition decision authorities and program managers prioritize cybersecurity risks to their systems, the challenge for OPNAV N2/N6 is to determine how to appropriately distribute investments across those risks—for example, by spreading investment across such areas as protection, detection, or response and recovery from cyber events.

## Challenges in Quantifying the Impact of an Investment

Finally, and perhaps most notably for the work described in this study, is the challenge of quantifying the impact (or return) of a potential investment. Business methods for assessing investments are not necessarily analogous to the defense context. This has been written about extensively, and we expound on it in this report as we describe our thought processes in arriving at our proposed framework approach. Typical business methods for valuing the return on investment (ROI) are monetized into (positive) cash flow, a concept that is only tangentially applicable to U.S. Department of Defense (DoD) investments to meet national security objectives, ensure operability, and protect lives. We also discuss how this is a challenge for investments that have already been executed as much as it is for potential future investments. This challenge is not unique to cybersecurity investments.

# Methods and Tools to Support the Prioritization of Cybersecurity Investments

The Navy has every intention of "building secure [information technology] services" (Weis and Stefany, 2021), but the space of potential risk is vast, budgets are constrained, and cybersecurity investments must compete with each other and with other investments that are unrelated to cybersecurity. In this section, we identify several tools and methodologies that OPNAV and resource sponsors use to help them work through the decision space. This is not exhaustive; there may yet be other approaches in use.

## OPNAV N2/N6

We highlight a tool that OPNAV N2/N6 uses to support its decisionmaking. It is only a part of the process, which typically involves scoring potential investments on a spreadsheet and conducting numerous meetings among the command over a period of months to decide on a set of investments for the POM.

### Force Level Integration Tool

The Navy uses a web-based tool called Force Level Integration Tool (FLINT) for prioritizing investments. FLINT is "a digital decision support solution that integrates disparate tools, models and subject matter experts . . . to optimize Navy Program Executive Memorandum (POM) decision-making" (Program Executive Office for Manpower, Logistics, and Business Solutions, 2021, p. 2).[2] FLINT incorporates a framework for scoring investments to support prioritization, which OPNAV has described as useful but also as something that can be improved upon. The framework proposed in this report is an alternative to that method.

## Resource Sponsor

We highlight the following approaches of three resource sponsors because they are similar in nature to the methodology proposed in this report. These resource sponsors use these approaches as part of their process to recommend investments. We did not ascertain the full process each of these three (or other) resource sponsors use to come to the set of recommendations provided to OPNAV N2/N6.

---

[2] FLINT is maintained by Naval Information Warfare Systems Command's (NAVWAR's) Program Executive Office for Manpower, Logistics, and Business Solutions.

## Naval Air Systems Command Cyber Risk Assessment

The Navy systems commands each have their own approaches to assessing cybersecurity risk. Naval Air Systems Command's (NAVAIR's) Cyber Risk Assessment (CRA) approach identifies potential threat vectors and the risks associated with threat vectors. NAVAIR combines this capability with a systems engineering cyberattack tree, which breaks down a weapon system (Kern, 2018).

At a high level, the NAVAIR CRA develops a cyberattack tree of a platform or weapon system by decomposing a mission into mission functions or systems and associated access points. It further analyzes these access points for the postures of attack surface, threat, and resilience (Burke and Morgan, 2018). This mission decomposition is often referred to as a *mission thread* and is rooted in systems engineering.

A mission is first broken down into mission elements or functions, with each function then decomposed into systems. The CRA also defines a functional flow among the systems and functions.

One of the products of the NAVAIR analysis is a set of cybersecurity risk matrixes that represent the cyber risk to the system. As shown in Figure 1.1, the system risk is a function of likelihood and impact, where likelihood is a combination of susceptibility and threat credibility, and impact is a combination of system tolerance and mission criticality (NAVAIR, 2019). CRA analysts determine susceptibility, threat credibility, system tolerance, and mission criticality using five-point scales based on several semiobjectively defined characteristics of the system and mission, such as cyber hygiene, supply chain exposure, system redundancy, and function dependency.

## Naval Sea Systems Command Cyber Vulnerability Assessment Tool

Naval Sea Systems Command (NAVSEA) has an approach called the Cyber Vulnerability Assessment Tool (CVAST), which identifies systems, subsystems, and components, along with test models to evaluate the systems' impact on a ship's mission and mission capabilities (GBS Group, undated).

## NAVWAR Cyber Figure of Merit

NAVWAR has a scorecard called the cyber figure of merit (CFOM), which, although it is related, is substantively different in approach. CFOM scores the cybersecurity health of an organization based on a set of questions (McDermot, 2019). For brevity, we do not expound further on these approaches in this report. NAVAIR's and NAVSEA's approaches require considerable knowledge about systems architectures to be useful, and while they are seemingly robust at identifying potential threat vectors and risks, are too low-level to be practically applied by OPNAV N2/N6.

These approaches are examples of how the programs and commands filter their investments before they provide them to OPNAV N2/N6 for prioritization in the POM process.

**FIGURE 1.1**
**NAVAIR CRA Risk Matrixes**

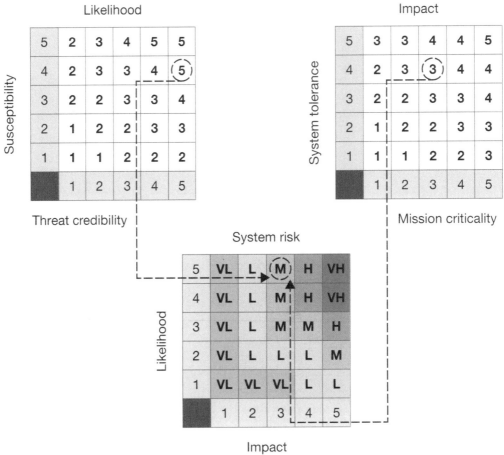

SOURCE: Adapted from NAVAIR, 2019, p. 4.
NOTE: VL = very low. L = low. M = medium. H = high. VH = very high.

# Relevant Federal Information Security Guidance

There is a voluminous amount of federal guidance on information security. Per the Federal Information Security Modernization Act, federal agencies are required to provide information security protections through a risk-based policy for cost-effective security (Public Law 113-283, 2014). The National Institute for Standards and Technology's (NIST's) Risk Management Framework is a mechanism created to satisfy those requirements, and it is DoD and DoN policy that the framework be used to implement cybersecurity requirements (DoD Instruction 8510.01, 2020). DoD Instruction 5000.90, 2020, provides policy guidance for acquisition decision authorities and program managers on prioritizing cybersecurity risks to their systems.

## NIST Cybersecurity Framework

In addition to the NIST Risk Management Framework, perhaps the next-most-visible (and relevant) tool for federal agencies to use to help prioritize and address the challenge of cybersecurity is the NIST Cybersecurity Framework (NIST, 2018). The framework was originally targeted to critical infrastructure and was later broadened in May 2017 to federal networks as a result of Executive Order 13800. Notably, the framework applies only to national security systems "to the maximum extent feasible and appropriate" (Executive Order 13800, 2017).

The framework "core" identifies five cybersecurity functions: identify, protect, detect, respond, and recover. A key aspect of the NIST Cybersecurity Framework is that it is not intended to be a checklist of actions but instead is intended to be a methodology for determining the cybersecurity stance for a given organization. It uses business and mission drivers interchangeably and strives to provide cost-effective cybersecurity risk management. However, it is not clear whether all five functions are relevant in all Navy contexts.

## NIST Special Publication 800-160

Where the NIST Cybersecurity Framework outlines cybersecurity functions, NIST Special Publication 800-160, *Systems Security Engineering: Considerations for a Multidisciplinary Approach in the Engineering of Trustworthy Secure Systems*, describes an engineering approach to system security (Ross, McEvilley, and Oren, 2018). This foundational document defines three contexts for security investment decisions: the problem context (i.e., What am I securing and from whom?), the solution context (i.e., What is my approach to addressing the security problem?), and the trustworthiness context (i.e., Does my security solution address my security problem as implemented?).

Importantly, the document differentiates the role of investments that assess system security trustworthiness, such as NIST's Risk Management Framework, and platform security features investments that are part of the security solution. Although this research and the resulting framework focus on analyses that support decisions in the solution context, a broader, holistic view can frame these decisions in the context of the threat and the economic and compliance landscape of DoN. The tendency when considering which cybersecurity investments to prioritize may be to focus on the solution context, where a holistic view of both the problem and trustworthiness are equally or even more important to the overall security of naval information technology (IT) systems. This might be the result of challenges related to upstream prefiltering, limited information, and comparing past- and future-year investments, or it could simply be the Navy's way of making a particular decision. Regardless, it is important to consider these other contexts to improve the rationale for investments.

# Approaches to Assessing the Value of a Cybersecurity Investment

Having discussed the motivation and challenges within the OPNAV N2/N6 programming portion of the PPBE process, the current OPNAV N2/N6 approach, and guidance for cybersecurity engineering, we discuss options for valuing cybersecurity investments. There are numerous options within the literature and in the private and public sectors. Within the Navy, organizations use various approaches. In the appendix, we discuss our review of the literature in this field, but in this section, we summarize our findings and how they informed our proposed methodology.

## Background

There are many accepted business metrics to compare alternative investment strategies, such as ROI, net present value, and internal rate of return. Although these approaches focus on the monetization of value (i.e., the economics of the investment), many of the investments OPNAV N2/N6 must consider are not conducive to monetization, particularly because it can be difficult to monetize a loss. Examples include the loss of a ship, aircraft, or information system availability, or the loss of confidentiality or integrity of data on a platform. Although there are some cases in which costs are avoided, for the most part, DoD investments provide a utility beyond a simple cash flow perspective.

There are yet other approaches that explore the value of a cybersecurity investment from a more–defense-oriented mission context. We explore and draw from a few relevant RAND research efforts in our proposed framework and discuss the methodologies later in this chapter.

## Information Security Economics

Despite the challenge of accurately monetizing value in the DoD context, information security economic approaches can be evaluated for their ability to inform the Navy's challenge by demonstrating concepts, data, and principles that can be factored into cyber investment decisions.

In the late 1990s and early 2000s, a body of research emerged that started to apply these concepts to IT systems, and particularly cybersecurity investments (see, e.g., Anderson, 2001). The information security economics literature (and accompanying empirical investigations) has developed numerous metrics, models, and processes for performing evaluations based on econometric principles.

Although numerous approaches now exist, at the heart of the information security economic literature are the following three key measurements:

- loss, or the value at risk were an intrusion, breach, or failure to occur (an extension of the consequence element of risk)

- vulnerability, which is generally expressed as a probability that captures the chances of realizing some or all the loss (an extension of the probability element of risk)[3]
- effectiveness or productivity of the investment in question.

Various metrics and models have been developed on these core concepts that attempt to capture and project aspects of the relationship between investment and cybersecurity outcomes. The remainder of this section summarizes this field; a more comprehensive treatment of these concepts can be found in Böhme, 2010.

## Economic Metrics

Information security economic metrics build on the core loss, vulnerability, and effectiveness measurements to develop indicators that can be used to quantify and track key aspects of investment. These measures form the basis for the most widely recognized set of econometric metrics focused on ROI, which seek to compare the current state with a projected state following some amount of investment. The most common basis for such a calculation is the annualized loss expectancy (ALE), which is defined as

$$\text{ALE}_x = p_x \times L,$$

where $L$ is the potential loss and $p_x$ is the probability (or risk) of incurring that loss within a period $x$ (usually over the next year; hence, annualized). The literature builds on the ALE by considering the delta, or change in the current ALE, to determine the earned benefit of information security (EBIS). This is an important concept we initially carried forward into our framework. We provide an example of the ALE, EBIS, and ROI for comparative security investments in the appendix.

Although ROI-based methods have a long history of application, they face several obstacles, the most common being accurate measurement of the key econometric concepts of loss, vulnerability, and effectiveness. Most importantly for OPNAV N2/N6 is the fact that monetization of loss is not relevant across all Navy investments.

## Economic Models

Numerous investment models have been constructed using ROI-based metrics; they attempt to overcome limitations and capture the salient aspects of cybersecurity investment in a way that permits accurate projection and analysis. These models might employ various underlying methodologies, using the identified metrics within different mechanisms to formalize and quantify the decisionmaking process. Because of the expansive nature of this literature, we focus on the most common model approaches relevant to the OPNAV N2/N6 mission: utility maximization and game theoretic approaches, which form the basis for much of the

---

[3] This may be endogenous (occurrence of exploitable weaknesses), exogenous (likelihood of an external threat), or a mix of both.

modeling literature. A broader view of this space can be found in the literature summary in the appendix and in survey works in the literature (e.g., Schatz and Bashroush, 2017).

## Utility Maximization Models

The most common and popular approach to modeling involves the application of econometric metrics within an optimization function to maximize the value obtained by a security investment. This approach is exemplified by the Gordon-Loeb (GL) model of information security investment, which was introduced in 2002 and is sometimes referred to as the "gold standard" information security investment model (Gilligan, 2013). Famously, the GL model was used to derive a fundamental limit on the amount of security investment of $1/e$ ($\approx 37$ percent) of the potential loss (under a strict set of assumptions) (Gordon and Loeb, 2002).

We conclude that, although the GL model is a powerful utility maximization tool, its dependence on the monetization of loss makes it very challenging to apply in the context of OPNAV N2/N6. Further information on the GL model can be found in the appendix. We provide examples applying GL to OPNAV N2/N6 data under different assumptions that highlight various challenges in a separate appendix that is not available to the general public.

## Game Theoretic Models

Game theoretic analysis, which is a complementary approach to utility-based investment decisionmaking, explicitly considers adversarial behavior as part of a mathematical analysis. Approaches in the literature provide insights that range from broad strategy to specific investment options, often over multiple investment periods, to examine security decisions in light of potential attacker retorts.

Many of the game theory papers (e.g., Schatz and Bashroush, 2017; Cavusoglu, Srinivasan, and Yue, 2008) take a strategic look, and thus might offer insight but not a process. However, this insight may not hold outside the context. Game theory requires not only adversary insight but a willingness and ability to create utility functions that are representative of the adversary.

Game theoretic approaches have relevance to the OPNAV N2/N6 prioritization context, however, as they often look to establish equilibrium, which is not maximization. The logical utility of game theoretic approaches is to use the results to inform the probability of attack, or $p_x$ in ALE. The extent to which this is considered in today's OPNAV N2/N6 approaches is likely limited to an ad hoc basis (e.g., decisionmakers believe that certain targets are more valuable and thus are more likely to be attacked than others). But without rigorous application, this approach is subject to numerous potential logical fallacies (e.g., bias), which can lead to suboptimal investment strategies. However, some game theory literature suggests that it is useful because many cybersecurity investment valuation approaches do not allow a security investment to influence the behavior of hackers.

## Hybrid Models

Although decision and game theory form the largest share of approaches in the literature, variations, extensions, and applications of these concepts have produced several investment valuation approaches. Numerous models can be found that apply the core principles described earlier to business processes, such as analytic hierarchy processes, to maximize specific decisions or outcomes; others apply different decision models, such as real options theory (Schatz and Bashroush, 2017).

Another approach is the development of hybrid models that unify different constructs. One such example is the iterated weakest link (IWL) model (Böhme and Moore, 2016), a multiperiod computational model that incorporates a game theory–inspired adversarial model in a computational construction. Rather than requiring the definition of defender and attacker utility, IWL assumes an attacker that will attack at the weakest link; that is, the point at which it is least costly to do so, which is known with some uncertainty. Likewise, the defender invests according to the same paradigm, which is again known with some uncertainty. The model supports defender investment as defenders seek to address enough attack vectors so as to leave any remaining vulnerabilities out of reach of the attacker. However, the uncertainty in both the attacker and the defender over which links are weakest creates situations that potentially lead to misinvestment (i.e., failing to apply investment to the weakest link). The model thus allows (1) defender investment considerations over scale and time and (2) attacker decisions to continue or abandon attack. In this way, IWL attempts to incorporate a more realistic attacker-defender interaction as part of the decisionmaking process. We provide an example applying IWL to OPNAV N2/N6 data under various assumptions in an appendix that is not available to the general public. As with GL and similar approaches, we find that applying such models as IWL to the OPNAV N2/N6 investment process is difficult, with little established theory and few examples to draw from in published literature.

## Cyber Insurance

Concepts that are analogous to the economic models include insurance in the private sector and options trading in the financial sector. We consider that the methods used by insurance companies to assess their customers' risk, and thus the concepts of loss and vulnerability, are potentially informative. There are two problems with leveraging insights from cyber insurance:

1.  Insight into how insurance companies price their policies is very limited.
2.  Insurance companies tend to consider only the compensation for an event, thus excluding the value of preventative investments from their approach.

An exploration of insurance carriers' security questionnaires provides insight into risks about which carriers are concerned (Romanosky et al., 2019). First, Romanowsky et al. notes an "emphasis on the amount of data (i.e., number of records) and the type of data (i.e., sensitive and confidential data) managed by the firm" (Romanosky et al., 2019, p. 11). This is useful for considering back-office DoN functions, but not operational contexts. Romanosky et al. further notes "little attention given to the technical and business infrastructure, and their interdependencies with environment," which is surprising because it is fundamental to DoN's CRA and CVAST approaches (Romanosky et al., 2019, p. 12). References to standards and frameworks (such as NIST) are nonexistent to rare, as are references to the size of an organization's IT budget.

We conclude that the cyber insurance market is perhaps too focused on commercial cybersecurity risks and otherwise is too opaque to be useful in mitigating OPNAV N2/N6's current challenges. That said, insurance carriers have to generalize over a wide variety of customers and attacks, which is analogous to OPNAV N2/N6 (if the various commands are considered customers), and their tactics reflect the challenge of quantifying security posture. This is something "that the information security industry has been struggling with for decades" (Romanosky et al., 2019, p. 18).

## Limitations to Information Security Economic Approaches

The limitations to the practical employment of information security economic approaches are a combination of well-known challenges related to quantified decision-support models broadly and challenges that arise in the application of econometric measurement and modeling. These limitations are as follows:

- **Stylization.** The tension between tractability and descriptive power is at the heart of successful model development (Varian, 1997). Complex models offer greater potential for precision and accuracy, but at the expense of computational, data, and understandability needs, which is a key challenge area for OPNAV N2/N6. Striking a balance requires the abstraction of some concepts and care in assessing the parameter sensitivity and output accuracy impacts.
- **Empirical basis and data availability.** Choices made as part of model development affect the type and amount of data required for valid operation. Requirements for accuracy and volume exist in both model construction, where valid parameter definitions rely on sufficient example data, and model operation, which requires the availability of specific data types and forms.
- **Scope and time.** Bounding the extent of investment considerations within any analysis is challenging, but the challenge is compounded when interconnected and evolving systems are the target. In addition to the technical challenge of defining system boundaries, results may vary based on the time frame under consideration. Tightly coupled to this is the common practice of discretizing investments and losses, which is sometimes referred to as a Bernoulli loss assumption (Böhme and Moore, 2013). Although this simplifies calculations from a distribution to a single-value estimate, it has the effect of creating snapshots tied to a point in time whose validity might be limited to specific circumstances.
- **Risk posture.** ROI-based calculations weigh outcomes equally, often combining many types of loss into a single parameter that is weighted equally against the investment. This reflects the economic principle of monetary fungibility and an assumption that losses are faithfully valued. As we discuss next, this may not reflect the scenario faced in

military investment, where such unmodeled, out-of-scope considerations as goodwill or political leverage could influence the desirability of different losses.

- **Optimality.** All ROI calculations seek to identify the point of optimal investment, or the "knee in the curve" that balances investment and return at maximum efficiency. Clearly, this often does not represent the maximal outcome, with model constructs reflecting accepted beliefs regarding the achievability of such attributes as security or effectiveness. Understanding these attributes is essential to understanding the expected result of investments at the level suggested by ROI models.
- **Impact of solution on vulnerability.** An often-overlooked aspect of ROI-based security investment is the impact of the proposed solution to the threat surface. Although any imposed change will affect the security posture of the investment under consideration, technical solutions (software and hardware additions) may suffer the same failures as the systems they purport to protect. As a result, these solutions offer the potential to expand the threat surface if they include weaknesses and vulnerabilities that are attractive to threat actors.

Looming over all the methods described in this section is the often-mentioned challenge of measurement. Although metrics for econometric investment using alternate measurements exist, few enjoy the attention (and level of examination) that ROI-based analysis enjoys. Base metrics, such as return on attack (Cremonini and Martini, 2005) and Cost to Break (Schechter, 2002), offer alternative ways to frame and perform quantified economic analysis, although research is required to further develop and validate these metrics into models and approaches that are suitable for broader employment. Although replacing or augmenting traditional ROI calculations with these metrics may address some shortfalls, any quantified approach requires careful application to understand inherent limitations and assumptions.

Despite these limitations, ROI-based methods offer approaches to information security investment that are grounded in quantified calculations, empirical analysis, and economic theory. Therefore, they provide a window into the problem of identifying security investments in the event that sufficient data and fidelity can be obtained and can be considered for incorporation into a broader Navy security investment decision support framework.

## Mission-Centric Cybersecurity Metrics

Another way of assessing the value of a cybersecurity investment is from a mission perspective. For several years, RAND has supported the Air Force with multiple cyber-related efforts. Two such efforts focused on topics relevant to the proposed methodology described in this chapter. Both take a mission perspective and focus on disrupting the adversary's attack path by increasing adversary effort and decreasing adversary benefit, which is somewhat aligned with a game theoretic approach.

## RAND Cyber Maturity Framework

Snyder et al., 2020, developed a cyber maturity framework (Figure 1.2) based on the adversary's (Red's) attack path.

To mount a successful attack, the adversary "must do four things: (1) access the system in question (access) *and* (2) know enough about it to execute an attack (knowledge) *and* (3) have the resources and capability to carry out the attack (capability) *and* (4) create an effect that has significant negative mission repercussions to the defender (impact)" (Snyder et al., 2020, p. 12). Noting that these adversary requirements are linked by Boolean "and" statements, Snyder et al., 2020, contends that, in theory, preventing any one of these four requirements would disrupt the adversary's attack path. In reality, cybersecurity defenses could reduce the likelihood of success of one or more of the parts, increasing the difficulty to the adversary of a successful attack and upsetting the adversary's cost-benefit calculus (i.e., increasing adversary costs and/or decreasing adversary benefits). Snyder et al., 2020, further breaks down each of the four components, at which point a maturity index can be defined based on whether countermeasures have been identified, implemented, tested, and found to work adequately.

## RAND Cyber Mission Thread Approach

A second cyber framework, developed by Snyder et al., 2022, focuses on decomposing a mission into a mission thread, like the NAVAIR CRA does. The report defines *cybersecurity risk* as a "combination of vulnerabilities to systems, threats exploiting those vulnerabilities, and the eventual impact to the mission(s) if the threat is realized" (Snyder et al., 2022, p. viii). However, the authors contend that, when prioritizing risk mitigations across multiple mis-

FIGURE 1.2

**Cyber Maturity Framework Using the Adversary's Cyberattack Path**

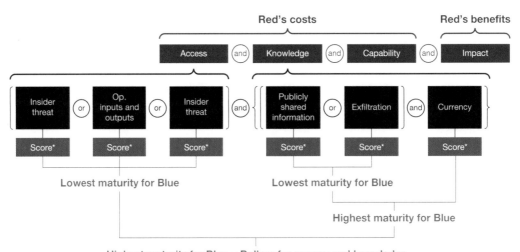

SOURCE: Snyder et al., 2020, p. 14.
NOTE: * Score represents maturity of Blue solutions to counter Red actions.

sions, it is infeasible to assess all system vulnerabilities and threats, and instead, some risk must be accepted in lower-risk areas. Thus, the framework focuses, at least initially, on assessing mission impact to determine resource prioritization for risk mitigation. The mission elements and systems in the mission thread are first triaged using graph theory to down-select those with higher criticality. Then, according to Snyder et al., 2022, a set of four criticality criteria that provide a proxy for mission impact are defined for each system, as follows:

1. The degree of system dependencies. Dependencies of systems on one another provide a measure of fragility of the architecture.
2. A concept we call *cyber distance*, which is the minimum number of hops of different protocols between the system of interest and a nonsecure network. Cyber distance provides a proxy for how accessible a system is in cyberspace and serves as an approximation of vulnerability.
3. A new concept we call *cyber separability*. Two systems are cyber separable from one another if no single cyber attack vector could simultaneously degrade the functionality of both. Cyber separability is a proxy metric for robustness to a cyber attack.
4. The relative (statistical) timing of an attack versus the (statistical) timing of a recovery, which provides a measure of whether the adversary or the defender has the relative advantage. Although not always easy to assess, when it is possible, the relative timing provides a powerful insight into the mission impact (Snyder et al., 2022, p. ix).

Once systems with high criticality scores are identified, further analysis can be performed to determine a risk mitigation strategy based on assessments of vulnerabilities, threats, possible mitigation investments, and their associated costs and effectiveness.

## Discussion

In this chapter, we discussed the motivation for this project and the challenges OPNAV N2/N6 faces in trying to evaluate and prioritize investments in the programming phase of the PPBE process.

We discussed OPNAV N2/N6's current approach to prioritization (in FLINT) and related efforts within the Navy, specifically CRA and CVAST (from NAVAIR and NAVSEA, respectively).

We introduced numerous cybersecurity investment valuation approaches that are common in the literature and used in industry and government. We discussed the limitations in implementing the information security economic methodologies in the OPNAV N2/N6 context: stylization, empirical basis and data availability, scope and time, risk posture, optimality, and the impact of the solution on vulnerability. We also introduced several RAND frameworks from work for the Department of the Air Force that we leveraged in the development of our proposed methodology.

## Informing Our Proposed Methodology

The challenges in developing a methodology for cybersecurity investment prioritization and decisionmaking in the OPNAV N2/N6 context are numerous. There is no silver bullet.

Calculations using ROI provide an "optimal" point based on the efficiency of the investment, or the best "bang for the buck." Although ROI-based methods have a long history of application, they face several obstacles, with the most common being accurate measurement of the key econometric concepts of loss, vulnerability, and effectiveness.

We conclude that, although GL and other such models are powerful utility maximization tools, they have multiple issues that make it very challenging to apply them in the context of OPNAV N2/N6—not the least of which is their dependency on the monetization of loss. We discuss some of these challenges in examples in an appendix that is not available to the general public.

Ultimately, the lack of information OPNAV N2/N6 has at its fingertips regarding the current cybersecurity state of systems (and systems of systems) and the potential impact of future and ongoing investments are key limiting factors in OPNAV N2/N6's ability to make informed prioritization decisions. Although complex models offer greater potential for precision and accuracy, this comes at the expense of computational, data, and understandability needs, which is a key challenge area for OPNAV N2/N6. In response to these challenges, we propose a qualitative risk-based approach for OPNAV N2/N6 in Chapter Two.

# Proposed Methodology

The proposed methodology outlined in this chapter was designed to address many of the limitations to information security economic approaches and challenges specifically faced by OPNAV N2/N6 (outlined in Chapter One). It is instantiated as a simple set of semiobjective risk scales that leverage important concepts from a subset of the current cybersecurity frameworks implemented across DoN and from RAND's ongoing work on mission-centric cybersecurity metrics.

For each investment, analysts are asked to assign a value from each risk scale both before and after the investment would be implemented. The difference between the two values for each scale is combined across scales to determine an overall risk reduction value provided by the investment. This risk reduction value is compared with the cost of the investment and the mission impact to inform investment decisionmaking and could be aligned with FLINT.

In this chapter, we provide a brief overview of the foundation on which our proposed methodology was constructed, present the approach, including the risk scales and implementation guidance, and finally, discuss the methodology's strengths and limitations. We demonstrate an example implementation of the methodology in Chapter Three.

## Foundation of the Methodology

The development of our methodology began with a review of a large cross-section of cybersecurity literature, including literature from information security economics (described in Chapter One), cyber insurance, and DoD mission-centric cybersecurity metrics; we also reviewed relevant DoN cybersecurity frameworks. We eventually narrowed our focus to a few documents that could inform a methodology to address the unique needs of a defense-specific approach (e.g., how to value mission benefits from an investment) and that was tractable within OPNAV N2/N6's timeline and data availability. Our proposed methodology was heavily informed by NAVAIR's CRA methodology (NAVAIR, 2019), and RAND's work on mission-centric cybersecurity metrics (Snyder et al., 2020; Snyder et al., 2022) (also described in Chapter One).

These three cyber risk frameworks, along with the NIST Cybersecurity Framework (NIST, 2018), formed the conceptual foundation for the proposed methodology outlined in this chapter. Concepts from each framework were integrated into relevant scales. The ability of the scales to capture the most important aspects from these frameworks (i.e., comprehensiveness) was also validated.

# Approach

Our proposed methodology is grounded on the idea that cybersecurity investments should be prioritized based on their ability to reduce overall cybersecurity risk to DoN; *cybersecurity risk* is defined as the expected impact to DoN missions from an adversary's actions through cyberspace.[1] Cybersecurity risk is often calculated as a function of vulnerability, threat, and impact (e.g., NIST, 2012; U.S. Department of Homeland Security, 2010).

## Simplification of Vulnerability and Threat

Given that intelligence on adversarial intent and capability (i.e., a component of threat) likely would not be available to OPNAV N2/N6 for cyber investment prioritization, we simplify this function to a combination of system exploitability and mission impact, where *exploitability* is defined as the ability of an adversary to exploit existing system vulnerabilities.[2] The term *system* in this definition should be interpreted broadly, because not all investments will be targeted to improve hardware or software systems. In fact, some investments will focus on improving personnel training or processes, which themselves have vulnerabilities (e.g., human error, lack of validated protocols). We therefore adopted the term *target of investment* (TOI) to refer to this broader class of investment targets more appropriately. The TOI could be quite broad and encompass many systems on many platforms.

## Proposed Prioritization Methodology

To prioritize investments in terms of their ability to reduce cybersecurity risk, our proposed methodology compares the (1) cost-effectiveness of an investment to reduce the TOI's exploitability with (2) the mission impact of a cyberattack on the TOI,[3] where cost-effectiveness is simply the delta in TOI exploitability (i.e., from pre- to post-investment) divided by the cost of the investment. This brings in elements of the information security economics approaches

---

[1] Note that we use the term *expected impact* to reflect the determination of an expected value calculated based on the probability distribution across all possible impacts.

[2] Understanding the difference between exploitability and vulnerability is crucial. Whereas vulnerability is a weakness to a system, exploitability is the ability of an adversary to exploit that weakness. The latter accounts for various circumstances that can increase the difficulty of an attack through cyberspace, such as an adversary not having the necessary knowledge to exploit the vulnerability or not having access to the vulnerable system or response capabilities that may reduce the likelihood of an adversary successfully completing the action.

[3] We discuss assumptions regarding this approach further in the assumptions and limitations section at the end of this chapter.

to ROI by capturing the delta in exploitability before and after the investment while eliminating the challenging aspect of monetizing the loss. Figure 2.1 shows a high-level depiction of this proposed approach.

On the left-hand side of the figure, investments are plotted on a 5×5 risk matrix, showing the reduction in TOI exploitability (i.e., the delta) for each investment on the vertical axis and the TOI impact on the horizontal axis. On the right-hand side of the figure, the relative value of these investments is shown in three dimensions: (1) cost-effectiveness of the investment (i.e., delta of exploitability divided by the cost of investment) on the horizontal axis, (2) mission impact of a cyberattack on the TOI on the vertical axis, and (3) relative cost of the investment shown as the size of the circle. For the latter dimension, while investment cost is integrated into the cost-effectiveness calculation, the overall size of an investment also might play an important role in investment decisionmaking. That is, generally, investments in the upper-right corner of this graph will provide a greater relative potential ROI (in terms of reduced cybersecurity risk). However, given that OPNAV N2/N6 will be managing a fixed budget, it may be advantageous to prioritize high-ROI investments that are also lower-cost overall. It is important to note that the impact score does not change before and after the investment.

## Risk Scales

To facilitate an estimation of impact and exploitability, we decomposed both components into a set of seven factors: two for impact and five for exploitability. All but one of these factors was further decomposed into subfactors. This decomposition was heavily informed by the mission-centric cybersecurity metric frameworks described in Chapter One (see NIST,

**FIGURE 2.1**

**Proposed Methodology for Prioritizing Cyber Investments**

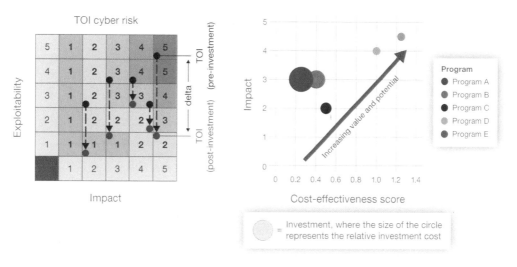

NOTE: Data shown are notional.

2019; Snyder et al., 2020; Snyder et al., 2022) and is shown in Figure 2.2. We assigned a five-point scale to each factor to further define the concept across an ordinal spectrum of semi-objective attributes of the TOI. These scales are meant to facilitate consistency of rating the factors and ensure that important aspects of cybersecurity are highlighted.

Tables 2.1 through 2.7 present the five-point scales for each cyber risk factor. These scales were constructed based on the assumption that investments ultimately are implemented to mitigate the loss of (or reduction in the) availability of critical mission systems or mission element functions, which could lead to mission degradation or failure. We briefly describe each factor in turn.

## Impact

These scales represent the severity of the impact of a loss of the availability of the TOI's mission element function. In other words, it attempts to address the following question: How important is the TOI to the overall DoN mission?

### Mission Importance

For the first of these scales, TOIs that are used more extensively across DoN (e.g., in multiple missions) or support more and higher DoN priorities (e.g., DoN, 2021, and urgent operational needs) would take on greater priority for investments.

### Criticality of Function to Mission

The second of the impact scales acts to prorate the level of priority based on how critical the TOI's function is to those missions. Criticality of the TOI's function, in this case, is represented by the mission impact if the function were unavailable. How much degradation would there be to the mission? How difficult would performing the mission become? The latter question is associated with the availability, accessibility, and effectiveness of mission-

**FIGURE 2.2**

**Decomposition of the Impact and Exploitability Components of Cyber Risk**

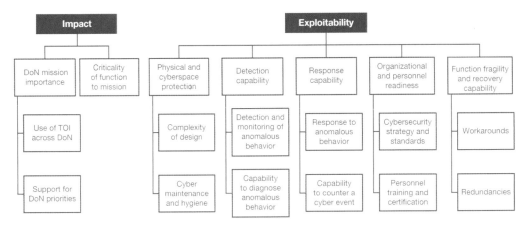

NOTE: DoN = U.S. Department of the Navy. TOI = target of investment.

TABLE 2.1
**Mission Importance Scale**

| Value | Level | Use of the TOI Across DoN | Range of TOI Support | Example Levels of TOI Support (at least one) |
|---|---|---|---|---|
| 5 | Very high | Extensive | Many of the highest of DoN priorities | • 4 or more CNO priority elements<br>• 4 or more urgent operational needs<br>• 400 or more ships or 3,100 or more aircraft or vehicles<br>• 1 million or more users supported |
| 4 | High | Considerable | Many OR high-level DoN priorities | • 3 CNO priority elements<br>• 3 urgent operational needs<br>• 142–399 ships or 625–3,099 aircraft or vehicles<br>• 10,000–1 million users supported |
| 3 | Moderate | Somewhat limited in scope | Some OR medium-level DoN priorities | • 2 CNO priority elements<br>• 2 urgent operational needs<br>• 41–141 ships or 125–624 aircraft or vehicles<br>• 1,000–9,999 users supported |
| 2 | Low | Limited in scope | Few OR low-level DoN priorities | • 1 CNO priority element<br>• 1 urgent operational need<br>• 12–40 ships or 25–124 aircraft or vehicles<br>• 100–999 users supported |
| 1 | Very low | Highly limited in scope | No DoN priorities | • 0 CNO priority elements<br>• 0 urgent operational needs<br>• Fewer than 12 ships or fewer than 24 aircraft or vehicles<br>• Fewer than 100 users supported |

SOURCES: Active-duty, reserve, and civilian numbers from fiscal year (FY) 2021 are from U.S. Department of the Navy, Deputy Assistant Secretary of the Navy (Budget), 2020. Contractor numbers from FY 2015 are from Cancian, 2019.

NOTES: We assumed 1,049,123 total active-duty (347,800 Navy; 184,100 Marine Corps), reserve (58,800 Navy; 38,500 Marine Corps), civilian (198,005 Navy; 22,896 Marine Corps), and service contractor (199,022 Navy) personnel. We also assumed 490 ships (all types) and 3,700 aircraft (2,500 Navy; 1,200 Marine Corps). CNO = chief of naval operations.

level workarounds (i.e., Are there other ways to perform the mission without this function?). Table 2.2. shows the proposed scale.

## Exploitability

The next five scales combine to evaluate exploitability. The use of self-scored scales with equal weight for protection, detection, and response reflects an inherent neutrality to these approaches. Accounting for preference in investment or establishing standards for capability assessment to reflect specific mission constraints is left to future work.

### Physical and Cyberspace Protection

This scale attempts to assess whether the TOI would increase an adversary's difficulty in gaining access to a system of interest and, if access is granted, reduce its ability to find its target (Table 2.3). Design complexity, in terms of heterogeneity, segmentation, and encryption, as well as patching known vulnerabilities through good cyber hygiene, can provide protections of this form. Routine cyber maintenance also can help reduce an adversary's knowledge about how to gain access to or find its target because earlier exfiltrated system information may no longer be relevant (e.g., because of system reimaging).

TABLE 2.2

## Criticality of Function to Mission Scale

| Value | Level | Effect of Performing the Mission Without the TOI's Function |
|---|---|---|
| 5 | Extremely critical | Likely mission failure OR impossible because mission-level workarounds for the function do not exist |
| 4 | Critical | Severe mission degradation OR extremely difficult because mission-level workarounds for the function have very limited availability, accessibility, or effectiveness |
| 3 | Somewhat critical | Moderate mission degradation OR somewhat difficult because mission-level workarounds for the function have some limits on availability, accessibility, or effectiveness |
| 2 | Minimally critical | Minimal mission degradation OR possible because mission-level workarounds for the function are available, accessible, and effective |
| 1 | Not critical | No mission degradation OR simple because mission-level workarounds for the function perform identically to the TOI's function |

TABLE 2.3

## Physical and Cyberspace Protection Scale

| Value | Level | Example Complexity of TOI's Design: Heterogeneity, Segmentation, and Encryption | Cyber Maintenance or Hygiene |
|---|---|---|---|
| 5 | Very low | Networked system with connection to the internet, no physical security or encryption | TOI is unsupported by vendor(s) and superseded by newer versions or product years, or operates with known critical vulnerabilities |
| 4 | Low | Networked system with internet | TOI is superseded by newer versions or product years or operates with known critical vulnerabilities |
| 3 | Moderate | Networked system using a noninternet protocol; limited physical security or encryption | TOI is supported, and security patches are applied within months or longer from vulnerability identification |
| 2 | High | Related system components are connected but air-gapped from other systems | TOI is supported, and security patches are applied within weeks to months of vulnerability identification |
| 1 | Very high | All system components are air-gapped from others, high level of physical security and encryption | TOI is supported, and security patches are applied within days to weeks of vulnerability identification |

## Detection Capability and Response Capability

These two scales assess whether the TOI improves the ability to monitor, detect, and respond to anomalous behavior through increasing frequency and autonomy (Tables 2.4 and 2.5). Once anomalous behavior has been determined and some immediate response is mounted, though, there is also a need to diagnose whether that behavior is a cyber event and, if so, counter it. These scales assess whether the TOI improves the capability to diagnose and coun-

**TABLE 2.4**

## Detection Capability Scale

| Value | Level | TOI's Detection and Monitoring for Anomalous Behavior | TOI's Capabilities (people, processes, and technology) to Diagnose Cyber Events from Anomalous Behavior |
|---|---|---|---|
| 5 | Highly immature | Nonexistent | Nonexistent or assessed to be wholly ineffective |
| 4 | Immature | Manual and completed at infrequent intervals or without standard operating procedures or updates | Minimal or assessed to be partially effective |
| 3 | Moderately mature | Manual and completed at frequent intervals with standard operating procedures; updates are infrequent | Deemed or assessed to be adequate but not fully comprehensive or modern |
| 2 | Mature | Semiautomated and updated as new vulnerabilities and attacks emerge | Comprehensive and modern but has never been assessed or assessment is not recent (1 or more years old) |
| 1 | Highly mature | Fully automated and updated as new vulnerabilities and attacks emerge | Comprehensive, modern, and recently assessed as sufficient (within 1 year) |

**TABLE 2.5**

## Response Capability Scale

| Value | Level | TOI's Response to Anomalous Behavior | TOI's Capabilities (people, processes, and technology) to Counter Cyber Events |
|---|---|---|---|
| 5 | Highly immature | Nonexistent | Nonexistent or assessed to be wholly ineffective |
| 4 | Immature | Manual without standard operating procedures | Minimal or assessed to be partially effective |
| 3 | Moderately mature | Manual with standard operating procedures | Deemed or assessed to be adequate, but not fully comprehensive or modern |
| 2 | Mature | Semiautomated | Comprehensive and modern but has never been assessed, or assessment is not recent (1 or more years old) |
| 1 | Highly mature | Fully automated, self-healing | Comprehensive, modern, and recently assessed as sufficient (within 1 year) |

ter cyber events through the adequacy, comprehensiveness, and currency of the technologies, processes, and people to perform these functions.

## Organizational and Personnel Readiness

The fourth scale used to evaluate exploitability attempts to assess whether the TOI would improve the readiness of an organization and its processes and personnel to prevent or mitigate the impacts from a cyberattack (Table 2.6). This is measured through the recency (and existence) of the organization's cybersecurity strategy and personnel training and certification. It is assumed that the quality of the strategy and training would at least meet existing regulatory requirements (e.g., acquisition programs would follow relevant guidelines in the program protection plan's cybersecurity annex) (DoD Chief Information Officer, 2021) and that these guidelines would be implemented to be applicable for the Navy's security context. Therefore, these guidelines may include assessments of—and processes and training for— such aspects as vulnerability identification and risk assessments; detection, response, and recovery procedures; and continuous improvement activities.

## Function Fragility and Recovery Capability

This is the final scale used to evaluate exploitability. It attempts to assess whether a TOI improves the ability to recover from a cyberattack by reducing the TOI function's fragility (Table 2.7). Fragility is measured in terms of the availability, accessibility, and effectiveness (to perform the function) of function-level workarounds and redundancies to the TOI's resource supply (e.g., power). The scale essentially asks two sets of questions. First, if the TOI were unavailable because of a cyberattack, are there other means of performing its function? If so, can it perform it as well and be accessed as easily? Second, if a resource supply for the

TABLE 2.6

**Organizational and Personnel Readiness Scale**

| Value | Level | Cybersecurity/Resilience Strategy and Standards (e.g., as part of a system's program protection plan) That Support the TOI | Cybersecurity Training and Certification for Personnel Who Support the TOI |
|---|---|---|---|
| 5 | Very low | Does not exist or is not documented | More than 3 years ago |
| 4 | Low | Minimally documented OR documented requirements are based on an outdated assessment (5 or more years old) | Between 2 and 3 years ago |
| 3 | Moderate | Mostly documented OR documented requirements are based on a semirecent assessment (3 to 5 years old) | 1 to 2 years ago but used out-of-date curriculum (3 or more years old) |
| 2 | High | Documented but based on an assessment that is not fully current (1 to 3 years old) | 1 to 2 years ago with up-to-date curriculum OR recently (less than 1 year) but used out-of-date curriculum (3 or more years old) |
| 1 | Very high | Fully documented and based on a very recent assessment (less than 1 year old) | Recently (less than 1 year) used up-to-date curriculum (less than 3 years old) |

TABLE 2.7

**Function Fragility and Recovery Capability Scale**

| Value | Level | Workarounds (e.g., people, processes, technology) to Perform the TOI's Function | Redundancies to the TOI's Resource Supply (e.g., power, people, information) | Example of Workaround/ Redundancy |
|---|---|---|---|---|
| 5 | Extremely fragile | Nonexistent | Nonexistent | N/A |
| 4 | Fragile | Limited availability, accessibility, or effectiveness | Limited availability, accessibility, or effectiveness | Manual workarounds with no failover or fallback capabilities |
| 3 | Somewhat fragile | Some limits to availability, accessibility, or effectiveness | Some limits to availability, accessibility, or effectiveness | Manual failover or fallback capabilities |
| 2 | Minimally fragile | Sufficient availability, accessibility, or effectiveness | Sufficient availability, accessibility, or effectiveness | Automated time-gapped failover or fallback capabilities |
| 1 | Not fragile | Perform identically to the TOI | Perform identically to the primary resource supply | Seamless failover or fallback capabilities |

NOTE: N/A = not applicable.

TOI is unavailable because of a cyberattack, are there other means of supplying that resource to the TOI? If so, can it supply the resource as well and be accessed as easily?

## Comparison with NIST's Cybersecurity Framework

As discussed in Chapter One, NIST's Cybersecurity Framework is the most visible and widely employed framework for reasoning about the challenge of cybersecurity (NIST, 2018). Therefore, to ensure the comprehensiveness of our exploitability scales, we performed a mapping exercise between NIST's framework and the exploitability factors and subfactors. Table 2.8 provides an overview of this mapping, with each factor and subfactor shown in the first and second column, respectively. The five primary functions of the framework (i.e., identify, protect, detect, respond, and recover) are added as the next five columns. Shaded cells in the table signify a mapping between the row's subfactor and the column's respective NIST framework function. We further decomposed this mapping to include the specific categories within each framework function (as outlined in NIST, 2018, p. 23). As shown in Table 2.8, the exploitability factors and subfactors cover the full set of NIST framework functions and categories, often with multiple framework categories mapping to one subfactor.

TABLE 2.8

## Mapping Exploitability Factors to NIST Framework Functions and Categories

| Factor | Subfactor | NIST Framework Function and Relevant Category | | | | |
| --- | --- | --- | --- | --- | --- | --- |
| | | Identify | Protect | Detect | Respond | Recover |
| Physical and cyberspace protection | Complexity of design | | AC, PT | | | |
| | Cyber maintenance and hygiene | | DS, MA, PT | | | |
| Detection capability | Detection and monitoring for anomalous behavior | | | AE, CM | | |
| | Capability to diagnose cyber events | | | AE | | |
| Response capability | Response to anomalous behavior | | | | AN, MI, CO | |
| | Capability to counter cyber events | | IP | | RP, AN, MI | |
| Organizational and personnel readiness | Cybersecurity strategy and standards | AM, BE, GV, RA, RM, SC | IP | DP | RP, IM | CP, IM, CO |
| | Personnel training and certification | | AT | DP | RP, CO | CP |
| Function fragility and recovery capability | Workarounds to perform function | | IP | | | CP, IM |
| | Redundancies to resource supply | | | | | CP, IM |

NOTE: AC = identify management and access control. AE = anomalies and events. AM = asset management. AN = analysis. AT = awareness training. BE = business environment. CM = security continuous monitoring. CO = communications. CP = recovery planning. DP = detection processes. DS = data security. GV = governance. IM = improvements. IP = information protection, processes, and procedures. MA = maintenance. MI = mitigation. PT = protective technology. RA = risk assessment. RM = risk management strategy. RP = response planning. SC = supply chain risk management.

# Implementation

In this section, we provide step-by-step instructions to implement the approach, along with important considerations for each step.

1. Identify the TOI. This could be a platform, system, component, enterprise resource, or capability.
2. Evaluate the impact of the TOI (all scores should be justified).
   a. Determine the Navy mission importance value. If the TOI is assessed to be different for the two subfactors, the higher of the two subfactors should be used.[4]

---

[4] Alternatively, the average of the two may be used. If this approach is chosen, the analyst should assess all TOI impact values in this way.

     b.   Determine the criticality of function to mission value.

     c.   Take the average of the two values. This becomes the impact score.

3.    Evaluate how the investment reduces exploitability.

     a.   For each exploitability factor, determine whether the investment is relevant (i.e., would the investment improve any of its subfactors?). If the investment is not relevant to a factor, do not assess it.

     b.   Calculate the delta score of each relevant exploitability factor.

         i.   Determine the starting value for the TOI by assessing the factor for the TOI's current state (before implementing the investment). If the TOI is assessed to be different for the two subfactors, the higher of the two subfactors should be used.[5]

         ii.   Determine the final value for the TOI by assessing the factor again, but now assume that the investment has been implemented. If the TOI is assessed to be different for the two subfactors, the higher of the two subfactors should be used.[6]

         iii.   Calculate the delta score (final value – starting value).

     c.   Sum the delta scores for all relevant exploitability factors; this becomes the exploitability reduction effectiveness (ERE) score.

4.    Determine the cost-effectiveness (in terms of exploitability reduction) by dividing the ERE score by the cost of the investment ($ millions). This value becomes the ROI-equivalent.

5.    Plot impact score versus cost-effectiveness.

6.    Repeat steps 1–5 for all investments.

7.    Prioritize investments with higher cost-effectiveness. For those investments with similar cost-effectiveness, prioritize by impact. For those with similar cost-effectiveness and impact, prioritize by those with lower actual cost of investment.[7]

## Mitigating Data Limitations

In our testing and validation of this methodology with actual investment data provided by OPNAV N2/N6, we found the data to be insufficient to assess the starting and final value (Step 3b above) for many of the investments. If this occurs, we provide an alternative for Step 3 below.

3.    Evaluate how the investment reduces exploitability.

---

[5]  Alternatively, the average of the two may be used. If this approach is chosen, the analyst should assess all TOI impact values in this way.

[6]  Alternatively, the average of the two may be used. If this approach is chosen, the analyst should assess all TOI impact values in this way.

[7]  Other investment prioritization strategies may be appropriate. The analyst should use the strategy that most reflects OPNAV N2/N6 objectives.

  a. For each exploitability factor, determine whether the investment is relevant (i.e., would the investment improve any of its subfactors?).
  b. Count the number of relevant exploitability factors; this becomes the ERE score.

## Assumptions and Tradespace Decisions

In any model development, the tension between precision and usability results in necessary trade-offs. When evaluating this methodology, it is important to recognize this tradespace and consider the limitations of the proposed framework in the context of choices and assumptions made in this specific framework or in this style of modeling more broadly.

### Key Assumptions

One key assumption we have made is that a cybersecurity investment cannot reduce the mission impact of a TOI. This assumption was made to reduce complexity, but in reality, it may not be true. As an example, a cyber investment might decrease response times by improving response planning or might improve recovery times by adding redundancy to a system. In both cases, the impact (specifically, the criticality of the TOI to the mission) may be reduced. These improvements appear to be adequately captured by the exploitability scale. The impact scale in our methodology better represents overall mission importance to DoN or mission-element importance to a specific mission (thread). And while investments could be made to alter mission-element importance (i.e., by altering the flow of a mission thread), we assume that the cyber investments that OPNAV N2/N6 will be prioritizing will not include such alterations.

Cyberattacks are often characterized as having an impact on system confidentiality, integrity, or availability (Nieles, Dempsey, and Pillitteri, 2017). For the purposes of this methodology, we assume that a loss of confidentiality or integrity of a TOI would result in the eventual unavailability of that TOI's mission element function. In the case of a confidentiality breach, this assumption presupposes that exfiltration of information about the TOI will eventually be used to adversely affect the availability of the TOI's function. In the case of a loss of integrity of the TOI, the assumption presupposes that the TOI will no longer properly support its function as intended, rendering the function unavailable. Although this assumption does not account for all adverse scenarios that could occur from a loss of confidentiality or integrity, availability was chosen to simplify the risk scales and focus on many of the most-severe mission impacts.

### Comparison with Information Security Economic Challenges

Relative to the broad challenges facing information security economic modeling highlighted in Chapter One, the proposed approach seeks to minimize the impact of these considerations and strike a balance between explanatory value and tractability. The limitations are as follows:

- **Stylization.** Most ROI-based calculations require insight into key attributes of both the investment under consideration and the operational environment. Such constructs as the impact and ERE scores provide tangible measures that make up complex notions of security, threat, and efficacy. However, as a consolidated metric, they run the risk of abstracting key details relative to the specific values and meaning behind these discrete elements. Separating out these terms would enhance model fidelity and accuracy, but at the cost of requiring more (and more-precise) measurements of these attributes.

- **Empirical basis and data availability.** Although limitations in the data available for model development affected the ability to perform model validation, continued use and assessment will improve accuracy and robustness.

- **Scope and time.** For the proposed model, it may be challenging to identify and bound the scope of the TOI, the mission impact, and its associated exploitability-reduction benefits over a defined time frame. This is closely related to the challenges identified previously related to the data and key elements of ROI-based analysis.

- **Risk posture.** Although the absence of a defined threat model simplifies model usage and calculation, it results in a challenge when seeking to incorporate explicit risk considerations. When coupled with a lack of weights on risk factors, this results in the definition of a de facto risk-neutral model. Changing to a different risk posture within the existing model could be accomplished by formalizing the establishment of model values such that they consider the user's risk perception, adjusting accordingly. Future work could better support this process through explicit model enhancements and/or complimentary processes and measures.

- **Investment type.** Investments under consideration can include one or more types of funding: research and development, procurement, operations, or maintenance. One area for future consideration is to think of these relationships explicitly as part of both the model and the decisionmaking process. This would necessitate more insights into such specific attributes as system security effectiveness and an understanding of how various investments affect those representations.

- **Optimality.** Care must be taken when employing optimality-derived decisions because they might not always lead to ideal results if the loss estimates do not capture the entire scope of negative outcomes—some of which may not be easily monetizable. Although this model reduces this effect by performing a relative ranking, future work could overcome this challenge in one of two ways:
  - The first would be to incorporate broader considerations (e.g., threat, severity, posture) to allow this optimization to be tuned more to DoN's needs, thereby factoring in nonmonetary (and potentially intangible) considerations.
  - The other option would be to move from an ROI basis to one that focuses more on defense metrics (beyond those currently implemented), such as return on attack. This

may change the nature of calculations, and the development of such a model would require further research and validation.

- **Impact of solution.** The proposed model does not explicitly consider impacts to the threat surface resulting from the addition of security solutions, although those impacts could be factored into the exploitability reduction delta score (Step 3b of the proposed process). Incorporating this aspect into the framework explicitly will require restructuring the framework steps but will separate the approach from contemporary decision-support investment models. Although it is not common for models to expressly incorporate the security mechanism as part of the security posture, it is important to note that many recent attacks have been enabled by adversary action against security mechanisms.[8]

In addition to these general challenges, specific trade-offs have been made to increase the usability or relevance of this proposed framework. These items collectively offer a roadmap for future work: in some cases, extensions to the present model; in others, unsolved research problems.

- **Measurement scales.** The impact and exploitability scores are categorical measures assumed to be linear, with movement along these 5-point scales resulting in the same magnitude of change; for example, the difference between high (4) and very high (5) in national security mission importance is mathematically equivalent to the difference between low (2) and moderate (3). Naturally, this may not be true in either the broad case or any specific case, and may be better served by a granular, weighted scale that allows the framework user to define the extent of change between values. At the very least, more work would better define and validate this aspect of the model.
- **Investments affecting impact.** The model construction considers investment effects only along the dimension of exploitability, not along impact. As pointed out previously, investments affecting attack impact could be considered within exploitability, a design choice that allows the impact parameter to capture on mission assessment. Employment of the NIST Cybersecurity Framework also places equal emphasis on reactive postintrusion actions as protective measures, such as the encryption of data at rest, rapid backup and reconstitution capabilities, or the rearchitecture of systems to remove critical data or systems from exposure. Explicit augmentation of this model through alternative security frameworks or constructs is an area for future research.
- **Life cycle coverage.** The proposed model does not explicitly consider all aspects of the TOI life cycle, lacking incorporation of supply chain, software design, and maintenance

---

[8]  For example, the "DoubleAgent" malware co-opts Microsoft Application Verifier to perform code injection (Newman, 2017), and famously, the SolarWinds attack targeted the Orion monitoring and detection capability by subverting a security technique for validating updates (U.S. Government Accountability Office, 2021). Some have pointed out that security products offer a rich target because of their privileged runtime status and the trust placed in them by users (see Xue, 2008).

considerations. Integrated treatment of these aspects is not common in singular invest-ment models because of both the underlying framework construction and the inher-ent complexity required to represent these multifaceted considerations. Future research into the balance of fidelity and representation could provide a pathway to one or more related models that capture a full life cycle view of investment (Snyder et al., 2015).

- **Objectivity of assessment.** Finally, although we were able to provide semiobjective mileposts (e.g., observable measures) for many of the risk scales, the establishment of many values for individual risk measures remains up to the subject-matter expertise and professional judgment of the user rather than objective assessment or evaluation. Driv-ing these aspects more concretely by data would increase the repeatability and objectiv-ity of the model, although the extent to which this is possible is limited by the fidelity and depth of data available. Although expert judgment can never be removed from such analysis, future work could investigate this balance for the purpose of generalizing the overall approach.

## Discussion

In this chapter, we presented a proposed methodology to prioritize cyber investments, given the unique challenges faced by OPNAV N2/N6. Informed by mission-centric cyber-security metric frameworks, the methodology uses a set of risk scales to determine the cost-effectiveness of an investment in terms of its reduction in exploitability and compares it with the mission impact of a cyberattack on the TOI if the investment was not implemented. The chapter presents a simple step-by-step process to implement the methodology, along with several areas for its further improvement. Like any methodology, the one presented here has its set of limitations. However, we contend that a simple methodology providing a first-order assessment of cybersecurity priorities that is actually put to use is better than a complex, highly accurate methodology that collects dust.

# CHAPTER THREE

# Example Implementation

In this chapter, we implement the proposed methodology using publicly available Navy budget materials from FY 2018 and FY 2020. We selected from the budget materials cybersecurity investments that are related to the types of investments OPNAV N2/N6 is prioritizing. We did not adjust dollar figures to all be in the same year's dollars because normally, this methodology would be used to rank programs from the same year. We used investments from multiple years because we could not find a single year with enough publicly available investment information to generate sufficient data points for this example implementation.

One challenge we have discussed is the sometimes limited information available that describes potential investments. The Navy budget materials are no exception, which makes it difficult to create a fully justifiable set of scores. However, to demonstrate the approach, we have created nominal before and after scores as best as can be determined from the available data.

We have implemented the alternative approach described in Chapter Two—where we count the number of exploitability areas the investment touches to illustrate how these two different approaches might produce different rankings—for just such limited data situations. The mission importance and criticality of function to mission scores are also a best attempt, given the amount of data provided, but ultimately, we were focused more on demonstrating the approach than on the precision of those two scores.

## Sample Investments and Scoring

### NAVSEA Boundary Defense Capability (Cybersecurity)

This investment focuses on protecting hull, mechanical, and electrical (HM&E) systems. Loss of HM&E systems means that a ship loses key capabilities, such as power and propulsion. According to DoN budget estimates for FY 2018,

> [t]he purpose of this effort is to define and develop enterprise Hull Mechanical & Electrical (HM&E) System cybersecurity solutions that will provide: protections from cyber-attacks such as boundary defense capabilities that will protect threats entering and leaving HM&E systems, physical protections, message authentication and encryption methods; Detection solutions for system anomalies and attacks at the boundaries, on hosts, networks and backplanes; and provide for operator awareness (e.g. malware

detection, file integrity verification, etc.); Reaction solutions that will enable operator and system responses to an attacks [sic]; and Recovery methods that will enable for a system to quickly get back to a good known state. Planning will also commence for the integration of cyber solutions into specific HM&E control systems (e.g., Machinery Control, Steering Control, etc.). (DoN, 2017c, p. 314)

The same budget estimates include the following on HM&E:

The development of a cyber-resilient HM&E architecture will include the integration of cybersecurity solutions and system engineering processes to individual HM&E Systems and their Components to ensure a consistent cyber security posture across the entire HM&E Enclave. Development of enterprise HM&E risk management processes will occur, to include the following: a vulnerability assessment and management process across the HM&E Enclave and a methodology to support the execution of the Risk Management Framework and Cybersafe Assessments. (DoN, 2017c, p. 316)

In Table 3.1, we show the scores for the impact scales.

We assigned a mission importance score of 4 because this investments cuts across a large number of ships and a criticality score of 5 because a ship cannot function without HM&E.

In Table 3.2, we show the scores for the exploitability scales.

Without knowing whether the HM&E upgrade includes air gapping, we cannot assign the physical and cyberspace protection scores a final score of more than 3; likewise, we do not know anything about the application of security patches, so cyber maintenance and hygiene also gets a 3. For the sake of this demonstration, we assume that the detection capability mentioned takes it from nonexistent to semiautomated and that the diagnostic capability goes from limited to adequate. We also assume that the response and counter capabilities go, respectively, from manual without standard operating procedures (SOPs) to manual with SOPs and from minimal to adequate.

TABLE 3.1
**NAVSEA Boundary Defense Capability Impact Scores**

| Impact | Score (1–5) |
|---|---|
| Navy mission importance | 4 |
| Criticality of function to mission | 5 |

TABLE 3.2
**NAVSEA Boundary Defense Capability Exploitability Scores**

| Exploitability | Description | Starting Score | Final Score | Alternate Score |
|---|---|---|---|---|
| Physical and cyberspace protection | Complexity of design | 4 | 3 | 1 |
| | Cyber maintenance and hygiene | 4 | 3 | 1 |
| Detection capability | Detection and monitoring of anomalous behavior | 5 | 2 | 1 |
| | Capability to diagnose anomalous behavior | 4 | 2 | 1 |
| Response capability | Response to anomalous behavior | 4 | 3 | 1 |
| | Capability to counter a cyber event | 4 | 3 | 1 |
| Organizational and personnel readiness | Cybersecurity strategy and standards | N/A | N/A | 0 |
| | Personnel training and certification | N/A | N/A | 0 |
| Function fragility and recovery capability | Workarounds | N/A | N/A | 0 |
| | Redundancies | N/A | N/A | 0 |

NOTE: Not all scales need to be scored (as indicated by N/A).

## LPD-Class Support Equipment: Shipboard Wide Area Network/ Consolidated Afloat Networks and Enterprise Services Integration

Like the HM&E boundary defense capability, the Shipboard Wide Area Network (SWAN)/ Consolidated Afloat Networks and Enterprise Services (CANES) investment focuses on improving onboard computer networks controlling HM&E capabilities. According to DoN budget estimates,

> [t]he results of the Shipboard Wide Area Network (SWAN)/Consolidated Afloat Networks and Enterprise Services (CANES) study directed the replacement of the [command, control, communications, computers, and intelligence (C4I)] capability of the LPD 17 Class SWAN with CANES and the conversion of the non-C4I SWAN into a new HM&E Network (mini SWAN). SWAN funding is required to field the new HM&E Network in support of the CANES installation. In addition, funding is required to sustain the legacy SWAN, while the LPD 17 Class ships await the CANES/HM&E Network back fit installation. SWAN serves as the backbone of the LPD 17 class and funding is necessary to address obsolescence, reliability issues, performance concerns, emergent Fleet requirements including enabling Cryptologic Log On (CLO), eradicating Windows XP, replacing aging obsolete network hardware (e.g., servers and core switches), and maintaining the Information Assurance posture of the Common Operating Environment (COE). This funding is vital to ensure the LPD 17 Class ships can combat the evolving cyber threat. (DoN, 2017a, p. 274)

For this investment, we found the impact and exploitability scores shown in Table 3.3.

We assigned this investment a mission importance of 2; although the LPD 17 class has only 11 ships, which would make it a mission importance of 1, it is an urgently needed investment. The criticality of the investment is 5 because, as with the previous investment, a ship cannot perform its mission without HM&E. Exploitability scores are shown in Table 3.4.

Because of the limited information available, we were able to determine only that this affects three exploitability criteria. We know that the CANES upgrade modernizes the network and is currently supported, but we do not observe any information about air gapping or how quickly security patches are applied. Bringing in more-modern equipment (e.g., CANES) would presumably mean that the cybersecurity standards are documented, but we do not know whether the level of documentation is better than it was with the legacy hardware, so we cannot assess whether there was an improvement on this scoring factor.

TABLE 3.3

**LPD-Class Support Equipment: SWAN/CANES Integration Impact Scores**

| Impact | Score (1–5) |
|---|---|
| Navy mission importance | 2 |
| Criticality of function to mission | 5 |

TABLE 3.4

**LPD-Class Support Equipment: SWAN/CANES Integration Exploitability Scores**

| Exploitability | Description | Starting Score | Final Score | Alternate Score |
|---|---|---|---|---|
| Physical and cyberspace protection | Complexity of design | 5 | 3 | 1 |
| | Cyber maintenance and hygiene | 5 | 3 | 1 |
| Detection capability | Detection and monitoring of anomalous behavior | N/A | N/A | 0 |
| | Capability to diagnose anomalous behavior | N/A | N/A | 0 |
| Response capability | Response to anomalous behavior | N/A | N/A | 0 |
| | Capability to counter a cyber event | N/A | N/A | 0 |
| Organizational and personnel readiness | Cybersecurity strategy and standards | 3 | 3 | 1 |
| | Personnel training and certification | N/A | N/A | 0 |
| Function fragility and recovery capability | Workarounds | N/A | N/A | 0 |
| | Redundancies | N/A | N/A | 0 |

NOTE: Not all scales need to be scored (as indicated by N/A).

# Ship Communications Automation

This investment targets cybersecurity improvements for ship communications, which allow a ship to communicate with the rest of the fleet and coalition forces. According to DoN budget estimates, this investment applies to

> [Military Sealift] Command (MSC) and United States Coast Guard (USCG) ships with a single shipboard variant. The ashore component of [Command and Control Office Information Exchange (C2OIX)] Project is the IP-based C2OIX Shore Gateway system. C2OIX will virtualize all Government Official Information Exchange System (GOES) software suites on shore gateway UNCLASSSIFIED, SECRET and TOP SECRET message enclaves and provide an integrated Cross Domain Solution (CDS) at the two Naval Computer Telecommunication Area Master Stations ([Naval Computer and Telecommunications Area Master Station (NCTAMS)] PACIFIC and NCTAMS ATLANTIC). C2OIX shore and afloat will satisfy Navy record messaging requirements and implement products that are developed with an open system architecture. . . .

> [Shore Tactical Assured Command and Control (STACC) Enterprise Network Management System (ENMS)] provides the mechanism for dynamic managed real-time information assurance, security and vulnerability mitigation within the tactical ashore networks. Network Management provides users with access to geographical real-time network situational awareness of cyber threats; and provides the operators the ability to understand what is and is not normal on the network and provide a pre-emptive cyberspace capability to fight and win in a cyber-denied information environment. . . . STACC transports Navy tactical data, providing seamless fail over and recovery capability. STACC requires that Automated Digital Network System (ADNS) and Computer Network and Defense System (CNDS) field in conjunction with STACC to provide a complete end-to-end capability from shore-to-ship and ship-to-shore.

> STACC's modernization plan is designed to eliminate cyber security vulnerabilities due to hardware and software obsolescence. STACC's systems are located in 5 regions, at 40 plus sites supporting the Fleet Commanders and their forces: 1) Eastern Pacific . . . ; 2) Western Pacific . . . ; 3) Indian Ocean . . . ; 4) European . . . ; and 5) Atlantic . . . ; and Joint and Coalition Partners within each region. STACC systems will also be procured in support of NCTAMS [ATLANTIC's] new integrated Communications Center. (DoN, 2017b, p. 444)

The complete explanatory submission for this investment can be found in the source budget document.

We provide impact scores in Table 3.5.

We assigned a mission importance score of 5 because of the large number of users affected and a criticality of function to mission score of 4 because of the severe degradation of the ability to achieve the mission that would result from a loss of communication. Exploitability scores are shown in Table 3.6.

We assign this as moving from a 4 to a 2 on complexity because it introduces enclaves into the system and from a 5 to a 3 on cyber hygiene because the TOI goes from having obsolete capabilities to supported capabilities. Detection reaches a 3 because, based on the statement about making the operator aware of anomalous behavior, it appears to be semiautomated; we would need more information to give it more than a 3 on diagnosis. Likewise, the reaction to and countering of cyber events seems to be manual and adequate, according to the information provided. Because the budget justification says that the capability provides seamless failovers, we score it as reaching a final score of 1 on redundancy.

TABLE 3.5

**Ship Communications Automation Impact Scores**

| Impact | Score (1–5) |
|---|---|
| Navy mission importance | 5 |
| Criticality of function to mission | 4 |

TABLE 3.6

**Ship Communications Automation Exploitability Scores**

| Exploitability | Description | Starting Score | Final Score | Alternate Score |
|---|---|---|---|---|
| Physical and cyber protection | Complexity of design | 4 | 2 | 1 |
| | Cyber maintenance and hygiene | 5 | 3 | 1 |
| Detection capability | Detection and monitoring of anomalous behavior | 5 | 2 | 1 |
| | Capability to diagnose anomalous behavior | 5 | 3 | 1 |
| Response capability | Response to anomalous behavior | 5 | 3 | 0 |
| | Capability to counter a cyber event | 5 | 3 | 0 |
| Organizational and personnel readiness | Cybersecurity strategy and standards | N/A | N/A | 0 |
| | Personnel training and certification | N/A | N/A | 0 |
| Function fragility and recovery capability | Workarounds | N/A | N/A | 0 |
| | Redundancies | 5 | 1 | 1 |

NOTE: Not all scales need to be scored (as indicated by N/A).

## Training and Education Equipment

This investment includes key cybersecurity upgrades, which are critical for performance of the mission—in this case, the training of Navy personnel. According to the DoN budget estimates,

> . . . [f]unding will support Enterprise Network refresh. The Navy Continuous Training Environment (NCTE) is a distributed training architecture and network that interconnects 111 Navy, Joint and Coalition training sites. To maximize return on the training dollar, reduce overall operating expense, and support the global live, virtual, and constructive nature of the NCTE, the suite of equipment must be continuously maintained, upgraded and keep pace with mandated [Defense Information Systems Agency] and DoD cyber information assurance requirements. Planned periodic replacement of hardware is essential to keep pace with technology upgrades, allow DoD mandated virtualization of the NCTE infrastructure. Virtualizing hardware systems reduces hardware requirements by consolidating hundreds of individual physical machines onto a much smaller number of virtualization server machines. This reduces Life Cycle Maintenance hardware costs, as well as space and cooling costs. Virtualization also improves resource availability by pooling computing resources and sharing them in response to real time demands. This means that instead of buying hundreds of computers that sit partially idle most of the time, the virtualization server is more efficiently utilized, reducing costs. The upgrades/ spare parts are vital to the Fleet's Live, Virtual, Constructive (LVC) training capability used by the U.S. Navy and Joint Services to prepare for deployment. Changes from FY17 to FY18 are: Increase of $2.499M is supporting planned hardware replacement of the NCTE infrastructure to ensure compliance with cyber security. Additional sustainment costs are due to requirements for increased cross domain information sharing needed for Carrier Strike Group (CSG) integrated training. NCTE Tier 1 hardware refresh/replacement includes routers, switches, firewalls and computers; network time servers; desktop/ servers/zero-clients to allow continued availability of services and comply with cyber security requirements including proxy firewalls and web proxies' requirements. (DoN, 2017d, p. 137)

Table 3.7 shows the impact scores for this investment.

Using the information provided, we found a Navy mission importance score of 2 because this training and education investment addresses one CNO priority element (readiness) and a criticality to function of mission score of 4 because the mission is not impossible without this investment.

TABLE 3.7

**Training and Education Equipment Impact Scores**

| Impact | Score (1–5) |
| --- | --- |
| Navy mission importance | 2 |
| Criticality of function to mission | 4 |

Table 3.8 shows the scores for the exploitability scales.

We assessed the training and education investment as reaching both a complexity of design and cyber maintenance and hygiene score of 3 because of a lack of information about how segmented the design was and how quickly security updates were applied. We gave it a 1 on cybersecurity strategy and standards because it appears to have been based on up-to-date assessments at the time, but this score could change if there were additional information clearly stating otherwise. Although personnel training and certification is important in making this investment possible, this was not an assessment of the training and certification enabled by this system, so we do not score it.

## Unix Servers

This investment brings cybersecurity upgrades and certifications to systems providing key support capability both for a large number of ships and other shipyards. According to the DoN budget estimate,

> [t]his project replaces [Norfolk Naval Shipyard's (NNSY's)] existing Corporate System (UNIX) Servers with Oracle/Sun Microsystems T-7 series servers, along with the associated support equipment, and 12 HPDL-560 Linux Servers and associated support equipment. The T3, T5140 and T5220 server platforms are part of the Corporate Server Datacenter Standard Architecture (CS/DSA) and have reached End of Life, and reach their End of Service support date in 2017, increasing cybersecurity risk. The servers are required to

**TABLE 3.8**

**Training and Education Equipment Exploitability Scores**

| Exploitability | Description | Starting Score | Final Score | Alternate Score |
|---|---|---|---|---|
| Physical and cyberspace protection | Complexity of design | 5 | 3 | 1 |
| | Cyber maintenance and hygiene | 5 | 3 | 1 |
| Detection capability | Detection and monitoring of anomalous behavior | N/A | N/A | 0 |
| | Capability to diagnose anomalous behavior | N/A | N/A | 0 |
| Response capability | Response to anomalous behavior | N/A | N/A | 0 |
| | Capability to counter a cyber event | N/A | N/A | 0 |
| Organizational and personnel readiness | Cybersecurity strategy and standards | 5 | 1 | 1 |
| | Personnel training and certification | N/A | N/A | 1 |
| Function fragility and recovery capability | Workarounds | N/A | N/A | 0 |
| | Redundancies | N/A | N/A | 0 |

NOTE: Not all scales need to be scored (as indicated by N/A).

run all mission critical and essential systems. This new equipment provides a technology refresh of critical shipyard systems. Replacement of this system is crucial to all NNSY overhaul and repair work, as well as work performed at the other Naval Shipyards, as NNSY centrally hosts selected Corporate Systems that are used by all shipyards. The ability to meet Cyber Security regulations and requirements is necessary to maintain accreditation and preclude disconnection. (DoN, 2017a, p. 403)

Table 3.9 shows the impact scores.

We rated the Unix server investment a 5 on both impact scores because it affects all shipyards and is critical to their ability to conduct their mission, given the statement that the system would be forced to be disconnected without this upgrade.

Table 3.10 shows the scores for exploitability.

We scored this investment a 3 on complexity because it lacks information on whether it improves the platform beyond modernizing the equipment; likewise, for maintenance and hygiene, it replaces unsupported hardware but does not say anything about how often the

**TABLE 3.9**

**Operating Forces Unix Servers Impact Scores**

| Impact | Score (1–5) |
|---|---|
| Navy mission importance | 5 |
| Criticality of function to mission | 5 |

**TABLE 3.10**

**Operating Forces Unix Servers Exploitability Scores**

| Exploitability | Description | Starting Score | Final Score | Alternate Score |
|---|---|---|---|---|
| Physical and cyberspace protection | Complexity of design | 5 | 3 | 1 |
| | Cyber maintenance and hygiene | 5 | 3 | 1 |
| Detection capability | Detection and monitoring of anomalous behavior | N/A | N/A | 0 |
| | Capability to diagnose anomalous behavior | N/A | N/A | 0 |
| Response capability | Response to anomalous behavior | N/A | N/A | 0 |
| | Capability to counter a cyber event | N/A | N/A | 0 |
| Organizational and personnel readiness | Cybersecurity strategy and standards | 5 | 3 | 1 |
| | Personnel training and certification | N/A | N/A | 0 |
| Function fragility and recovery capability | Workarounds | N/A | N/A | 0 |
| | Redundancies | N/A | N/A | 0 |

NOTE: Not all scales need to be scored (as indicated by N/A).

software will be updated. We would need more information to give this a better score than 3 on strategy and standards.

## LSD HM&E Cyber Resiliency

This investment funds HM&E cybersecurity improvements for the LSD-41–class ships. According to the DoN budget estimate, this investment is for

> HM&E cyber resiliency shipalts on LSD-41 class ships. The shipalts would each include a Boundary Defense Capability (BDC), a central HM&E Situational Awareness (SA) tool, TAPs into HM&E data flow and weasel boards on the backplanes of select HM&E equipment providing the capabilities required to detect anomalous activity, react by segmenting the shipboard network and restore to normal operating conditions. (DoN, 2019a, p. 825)

We provide impact scores for this investment in Table 3.11.

We rank these cyber resiliency improvements as a mission importance of 2; although there are only a handful of LSD-41–class ships, this is an urgent operational need. The criticality of function to the mission score is 4 because it is not clear whether the mission would completely fail without this upgrade.

Exploitability scores are provided in Table 3.12.

We use the boundary defense capability to justify scoring this a 3 on complexity of design, but that is the only piece of information given that is relevant to the physical and cyberspace protection scales. The other tools listed justify a 3 on the detection and response capability scales. We would need to know more, such as whether there is automation of detection and response, to score these higher.

## DDG 1000–Class HM&E Product Improvement

This investment supports hardware and software upgrades to integrate the Total Ship Computing Environment for DDG 1000–class ships. According to the DoN budget estimates,

> The Total Ship Computing Environment (TSCE) integrates all the ship's sensors and weapons into a cohesive Combat System (CS). The TSCE is integrated with an array of sensors and weapons that exchange data across the domains with the core network using a series of buffering computers known as Distributed Adaptation Processors (DAPs). The new ZUMWALT Class ship design has reliable and effective land-attack maritime dominance capabilities that meet stringent signature goals, which are interoperable with Joint forces.
>
> Funding required for hardware procurement and hardware engineering support to support Windows 10 Upgrade, Linux Kernel Integrity Validation tool, and Secure Data Distribution Services equipment. Windows 10 upgrade is required to support existing capabilities, prevent cybersecurity vulnerabilities, and is mandated by OPNAV requirements. Installation of Linux Kernel Integrity Validation tool will upgrade methods for detect-

TABLE 3.11
## LSD HM&E Cyber Resiliency Impact Scores

| Impact | Score (1–5) |
| --- | --- |
| Navy mission importance | 2 |
| Criticality of function to mission | 4 |

TABLE 3.12
## LSD HM&E Cyber Resiliency Exploitability Scores

| Exploitability | Description | Starting Score | Final Score | Alternate Score |
| --- | --- | --- | --- | --- |
| Physical and cyberspace protection | Complexity of design | 5 | 3 | 1 |
| | Cyber maintenance and hygiene | N/A | N/A | 0 |
| Detection capability | Detection and monitoring of anomalous behavior | 5 | 3 | 1 |
| | Capability to diagnose anomalous behavior | 5 | 3 | 1 |
| Response capability | Response to anomalous behavior | 5 | 3 | 1 |
| | Capability to counter a cyber event | 5 | 3 | 1 |
| Organizational and personnel readiness | Cybersecurity strategy and standards | N/A | N/A | 0 |
| | Personnel training and certification | N/A | N/A | 0 |
| Function fragility and recovery capability | Workarounds | N/A | N/A | 0 |
| | Redundancies | N/A | N/A | 0 |

ing malicious activity (including "Zero-day" attacks) in order to keep pace with ongoing threats. Secure Data Distribution Services will provide comprehensive detection and countermeasure capabilities to ensure data confidentiality and integrity, and will help keep pace with ongoing threats. . . .

FY20 [Other Procurement, Navy] funding is required to procure ZUMWALT Class ships network and computing equipment to address obsolescence and [Diminishing Manufacturing Sources] concerns to sustain the ZUMWALT Class TSCE and minimize total operation costs. Fifty percent of TSCE components are currently obsolete and obsolescence forecasts predict ninety percent obsolete by FY20. NRE is based on SD-22 solution costs adjusted for inflation for current and predicted obsolescence. Funding is required to maintain ship readiness; without funding, obsolescence in ZUMWALT Class network and computing environments will impact the ship's ability to get underway, increase cybersecurity vulnerabilities, and decrease capacity for sparing. (DoN, 2019a, p. 530)

Table 3.13 shows the impact scores.

We rank these upgrades as a mission importance of 2; although there are only three DDG 1000–class ships, this is an urgent operational need. The criticality of function to the mission score is 5 because of the necessity of the upgrades for the DDG 1000 class.

Exploitability scores are provided in Table 3.14.

We scored this investment as a 2 on complexity of design because it adds some segmentation to the network but scored it a 3 on cyber maintenance and hygiene because it replaces unsupported hardware and software but does not say anything about how often the software will be updated. We give it a 3 on both detection capabilities and the capability to counter a cyber event because the budget estimate does not say how automated the process is. We would need more information about the diagnostic capabilities to give it more than a 3.

TABLE 3.13

**DDG 1000–Class HM&E Product Improvement Impact Scores**

| Impact | Score (1–5) |
|---|---|
| Navy mission importance | 2 |
| Criticality of function to mission | 5 |

TABLE 3.14

**DDG 1000–Class HM&E Product Improvement Exploitability Scores**

| Exploitability | Description | Starting Score | Final Score | Alternate Score |
|---|---|---|---|---|
| Physical and cyberspace protection | Complexity of design | 5 | 2 | 1 |
| | Cyber maintenance and hygiene | 5 | 3 | 1 |
| Detection capability | Detection and monitoring of anomalous behavior | 5 | 3 | 1 |
| | Capability to diagnose anomalous behavior | 5 | 3 | 1 |
| Response capability | Response to anomalous behavior | N/A | N/A | 0 |
| | Capability to counter a cyber event | 5 | 3 | 1 |
| Organizational and personnel readiness | Cybersecurity strategy and standards | 5 | 3 | 1 |
| | Personnel training and certification | N/A | N/A | 0 |
| Function fragility and recovery capability | Workarounds | N/A | N/A | 0 |
| | Redundancies | N/A | N/A | 0 |

# CVN Cybersecurity

This project funds the installation of boundary defense capabilities on CVN Nimitz–class ships and necessary cybersecurity standards compliance upgrades.

> CVN Cyber Security enables the development and installation of Ship Change Documents (SCDs) for Boundary Defense Capability (BDC), Situational Awareness and Physical Security. It will increase the Defense in Depth and improve the Cyber Security aspects of the CVN Nimitz Class HM&E Networks. Funding will be used to update hardware and software applications and system configurations required to be compatible with and meet DoD CYBER requirements, Security Technical Implementation Guide and other CYBER requirements. Funding will also be used to update system cybersecurity Certification and Accreditation. Add capability to protect, detect, and respond/recover to internal system events, and add additional defense in depth and monitoring to external interfaces. (DoN, 2019a, p. 614)

> Funds were added in FY19 to provide cybersecurity of carrier assets and infrastructure with emphasis to prevent network intrusion on CVNs. Efforts consists [sic] of (1) boundary defense mods, (2) situational awareness mods and (3) physical security mods. Quantities vary per hull and are fundamentally different; therefore not shown since not suited for comparison. Hulls will receive different mods in varying combinations; so each hull cost is mutually exclusive of others [sic] costs. $8M Cybersecurity increase from FY19 to FY20 due to phasing of Cybersecurity solutions for CVNs and current maintenance/modernization availability schedule. Two hulls scheduled for Cybersecurity upgrades in FY20 compared to one hull in FY19. (DoN, 2019a, p. 619)

We provide impact scores in Table 3.15.

This program receives a 2 on Navy mission importance because it touches fewer than 12 ships but meets an urgent operational need. We give it a 5 on criticality of function to mission because of the need to stay current with cybersecurity accreditations.

Exploitability scores are provided in Table 3.16.

This program receives scores of 3 in the physical and cyberspace protection areas because of a lack of discussion about segmentation of the network and frequency of the application of updates going forward. It receives scores of 3 in the detection capabilities because there is no discussion of how automated the capabilities are or how recent the assessment or modernity of these upgrades are. It also receives scores of 3 in the response capability categories for the same reasons. We would likewise need more information about how recent the cybersecurity strategy and standards being targeted are in order to give better than a 3 on that scale.

TABLE 3.15

## CVN Cybersecurity Impact Scores

| Impact | Score (1–5) |
| --- | --- |
| Navy mission importance | 2 |
| Criticality of function to mission | 5 |

TABLE 3.16

## CVN Cybersecurity Exploitability Scores

| Exploitability | Description | Starting Score | Final Score | Alternate Score |
|---|---|---|---|---|
| Physical and cyberspace protection | Complexity of design | 5 | 3 | 1 |
| | Cyber maintenance and hygiene | 5 | 3 | 1 |
| Detection capability | Detection and monitoring of anomalous behavior | 5 | 3 | 1 |
| | Capability to diagnose anomalous behavior | 5 | 3 | 1 |
| Response capability | Response to anomalous behavior | 5 | 3 | 1 |
| | Capability to counter a cyber event | 5 | 3 | 1 |
| Organizational and personnel readiness | Cybersecurity strategy and standards | 5 | 3 | 1 |
| | Personnel training and certification | N/A | N/A | 0 |
| Function fragility and recovery capability | Workarounds | N/A | N/A | 0 |
| | Redundancies | N/A | N/A | 0 |

# Cyber Operations Technology Development

This investment funds improvements for Marine Corps Cyber Mission Forces, such as improvements to the Marine Corps Enterprise Network. According to the DoN budget estimate,

> [t]his program element supports cost associated with research, development, and modification of cyber technologies supporting Marine Corps Cyber Mission Forces (CMF) and missions assigned by USCYBERCOM.

> The Strategic Cyber Security Operations Development is an initiative to conduct engineering and manufacturing development tasks aimed at the attainment and maintenance of the security properties of the Marine Corps and its assets against relevant security risks within the cyber environment. This project includes cyber security tools system development, integration, enhancement and demonstrations designed at protecting and defending the Marine Corps Enterprise Network (MCEN); defending national interests against cyberattacks of significant consequence; and providing integrated cyber capabilities to support military operations and contingency plans. The project incorporates development of strategic partnerships with defense intelligence agencies and commercial cyber security developers in order to leverage current and emerging cyber security technologies in defensive/offensive tools, policies, security concepts, security safeguards, guidelines, risk management approaches, actions, training, and best practices that can be used to protect the Marine Corps' cyber domain; organization and user's assets. Marine Corps' organization and user's assets include connected computing devices, infrastructure, applica-

tions, services, telecommunications systems, and the totality of transmitted and/or stored information in the cyber environment. (DoN, 2019b, p. 2107)

Impact scores are provided in Table 3.17.

We rank this investment a 4 on Navy mission importance on the assumption that this TOI supports 10,000 to 1 million users. We rate it a 2 on criticality; we do not have sufficient information to assume more than minimal mission degradation should this TOI be made unavailable because of a cyber event.

Exploitability scores are provided in Table 3.18.

We ranked this investment as going from a 4 to a 3 on cyber maintenance and hygiene and from a 3 to a 2 on ability to diagnose cyber events from anomalous behavior. However, both of these scores required a high degree of subjective interpretation on the part of the authors in order to be able to score even these two exploitability dimensions. This was because the investment seemingly targeted many TOIs and because of overall vagueness in what the investment is producing. We included this example to highlight that these sorts of investment descriptions will need to be contended with when implementing our methodology.

**TABLE 3.17**

## Cyber Operations Technology Development Impact Scores

| Impact | Score (1–5) |
|---|---|
| Navy mission importance | 4 |
| Criticality of function to mission | 2 |

**TABLE 3.18**

## Cyber Operations Technology Development Exploitability Scores

| Exploitability | Description | Starting Score | Final Score | Alternate Score |
|---|---|---|---|---|
| Physical and cyberspace protection | Complexity of design | N/A | N/A | 0 |
| | Cyber maintenance and hygiene | 4 | 3 | 1 |
| Detection capability | Detection and monitoring of anomalous behavior | N/A | N/A | 0 |
| | Capability to diagnose anomalous behavior | 3 | 2 | 1 |
| Response capability | Response to anomalous behavior | N/A | N/A | 0 |
| | Capability to counter a cyber event | N/A | N/A | 0 |
| Organizational and personnel readiness | Cybersecurity strategy and standards | N/A | N/A | 0 |
| | Personnel training and certification | N/A | N/A | 0 |
| Function fragility and recovery capability | Workarounds | N/A | N/A | 0 |
| | Redundancies | N/A | N/A | 0 |

# Assessments and Evaluations of Cyber Vulnerabilities

This investment funds such cybersecurity exercises as Vulnerability Assessment Reports, Cyber Table Top Exercises, and Cyber Risk Analysis. According to the DoN budget estimate,

> This effort provides an [Operational Test and Evaluation] approach to protect Marine Corps critical Cyber information and intelligence through vulnerability evaluations of all major DoD weapons systems and critical military installations; as directed by Section 1650 of Public Law 114-328 ([National Defense Authorization Act (NDAA)] for FY2017) and Section 1647 of Public Law 114-92 (NDAA FY2016). This will be accomplished through protection, detection, response, restoration, remediation, and mitigation. Testing and evaluation will be completed at Marine Corps facilities and Government Labs, to include the Marine Corps Cyber Range, Naval Air Systems Command (NAVAIR) and Marine Corps Tactical Systems Support Activity (MCTSSA).
>
> Sec. 1647 of the FY16 NDAA directs the Secretary of Defense to complete an evaluation of the cyber vulnerabilities of each major weapon system of the Department of Defense by not later than December 31, 2019. Funded vulnerability assessments will build upon existing efforts regarding the identification and mitigation of cyber vulnerabilities of major weapons systems, and shall not duplicate similar ongoing efforts such as Task Force Cyber Awakening or conduct redundant assessment on systems that have already been evaluated.
>
> Sec. 1647 assessment will be formalized in Vulnerability Assessment Reports (VARs), Cyber Table Top Exercises (CTTXs), Cyber Risk Analysis (CRAs) and other reporting.
>
> Sec. 1650 of the FY17 NDAA directs the Secretary of Defense to submit a plan for assessing the cyber vulnerability of critical defense infrastructure and begin assessment of this infrastructure during a preliminary pilot program that will assess no fewer than two installations by December, 31 2019. Assessments will end in 2020 with the submission of the final report. Strategies mitigating the risk of cyber vulnerabilities should be identified during the course of evaluation. (DoN, 2019c, p. 377)

Impact scores for this investment are provided in Table 3.19.

We rank this investment as a 5 on Navy mission importance on the assumption that it touches four or more urgent operational needs. We rank it a 1 on criticality of function to mission because there is no indication that not funding this investment would directly result in an inability to perform any Navy missions.

TABLE 3.19

**Assessments and Evaluations of Cyber Vulnerabilities Impact Scores**

| Impact | Score (1–5) |
| --- | --- |
| Navy mission importance | 5 |
| Criticality of function to mission | 1 |

Exploitability scores are provided in Table 3.20.

We score this as going from a 3 to a 2 on cyber maintenance and hygiene on the assumptions that these exercises have most recently been conducted multiple months prior and that funding the investment will reset the clock on how long it has been since these exercises have been conducted.

## Ranking the Investments

We next plot the impact and cost-effectiveness of each investment using their starting and final scores, as shown in Figure 3.1.

As discussed in Chapter Two, the relative value of these investments is shown in three dimensions: (1) cost-effectiveness of the investment (i.e., delta of exploitability divided by the cost of investment) on the horizontal axis, (2) mission impact of a cyberattack on the TOI on the vertical axis, and (3) relative cost of the investment shown as the size of the circle.

If there is limited information available about the baseline (starting score), then we can use the alternative scoring method shown in Figure 3.2.

In both cases, the NAVSEA boundary defense investment is the top pick for the highest cost-effectiveness of the group and the Unix servers replacement comes second. The primary difference is that, when we use the baseline scoring (before and after) method for exploitability scores, the assessments and evaluations of cyber vulnerabilities investment is between the cyber operations technology development and training equipment investments, whereas in the alternative method, the latter two have almost identical scores, meaning that the training

**TABLE 3.20**

**Cyber Operations Technology Development Exploitability Scores**

| Exploitability | Description | Starting Score | Final Score | Alternate Score |
|---|---|---|---|---|
| Physical and cyberspace protection | Complexity of design | N/A | N/A | 0 |
| | Cyber maintenance and hygiene | 3 | 2 | 1 |
| Detection capability | Detection and monitoring of anomalous behavior | N/A | N/A | 0 |
| | Capability to diagnose anomalous behavior | N/A | N/A | 0 |
| Response capability | Response to anomalous behavior | N/A | N/A | 0 |
| | Capability to counter a cyber event | N/A | N/A | 0 |
| Organizational and personnel readiness | Cybersecurity strategy and standards | N/A | N/A | 0 |
| | Personnel training and certification | N/A | N/A | 0 |
| Function fragility and recovery capability | Workarounds | N/A | N/A | 0 |
| | Redundancies | N/A | N/A | 0 |

FIGURE 3.1

## Impact and Cost-Effectiveness of the Sample Investments

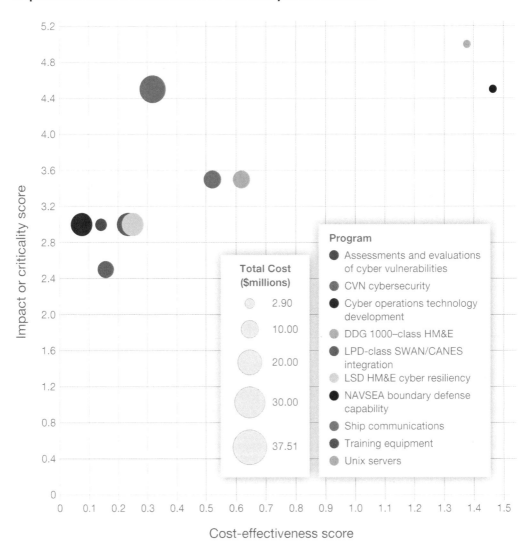

equipment investment gets scored significantly lower on cost-effectiveness. The other main difference is that the ship communications investment scores a lot lower on cost-effectiveness in the alternative method.

We did not rank-order the investments based on a function of cost-effectiveness and impact because in its current state, this framework is more of a decision aid than a definitive conclusion.

FIGURE 3.2

**Alternative Impact and Cost-Effectiveness of the Sample Investments**

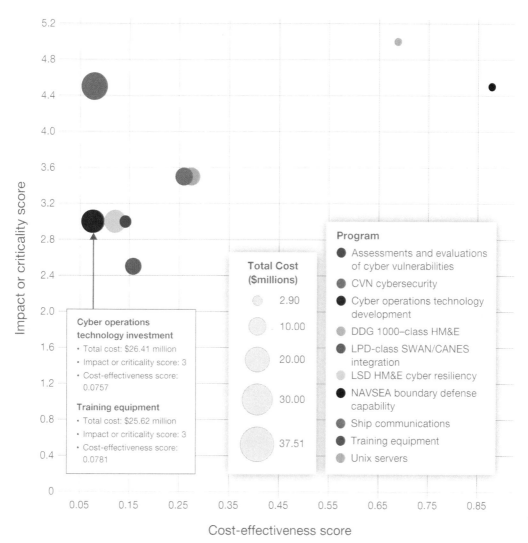

## Discussion

In this chapter, we showed an example implementation of the baseline (before and after) and alternate scoring methods using a selection of five sample investments from FY 2018 and FY 2020 Navy budget documents. We selected a variety of investment types to show how this methodology can be used to produce a single ranking of very different types of investments. This example implementation also demonstrates that while—ideally—there would be enough information to do the delta rankings, the alternate scoring may produce results that are not significantly different from the delta scoring. Further study of the differences between the two scoring methods would be useful.

# CHAPTER FOUR

# Conclusions, Recommendations, and Next Steps

The challenges in developing a methodology for cybersecurity investment prioritization and decisionmaking in the OPNAV N2/N6 context are numerous. There is no silver bullet.

## Information Security Economic Approaches Are Not Directly Applicable

Calculations using ROI provide an "optimal" point based on the efficiency of the investment—the best "bang for the buck." Although ROI-based methods have a long history of application, they face several obstacles, the most common being accurate measurement of the key econometric concepts of loss, vulnerability, and effectiveness.

We conclude that, although such models as GL are powerful utility maximization tools, they have multiple issues that make it very challenging to apply them in the context of OPNAV N2/N6—not the least of which is their dependency on the monetization of loss. Ultimately, the lack of information OPNAV N2/N6 has at its fingertips regarding the current cybersecurity state of systems and the potential impact of future and ongoing investments are key limiting factors in OPNAV N2/N6's ability to use complex ROI approaches to rationalize between investment prioritization decisions. Although complex ROI models offer greater potential for precision and accuracy, it comes at the expense of computational, data, and understandability needs, which are a key challenge area for OPNAV N2/N6. It is because of these challenges that we arrived at the approach proposed in this report.

## Approach

Our alternate methodology provides OPNAV N2/N6 with an additional tool to pilot and consider within the PPBE process to help it understand and prioritize cybersecurity investments. The methodology brings elements of information security economics literature, mission-centric cybersecurity metrics, and existing DoN approaches to cybersecurity risk assessment, within the context of a practical implementation scheme to provide an approach to informing the relative cost-effectiveness of investments. We note that approaches rooted in information security economics require insight into the losses, vulnerability, and efficiency involved with the investment and TOI. Although some uncertainty in these measurements is to be expected, an inability to estimate these attributes, partly because of the challenges OPNAV N2/N6 faces in the process, leads to imprecise calculations of utility. Out of practicality, we avoid the monetary quantification of loss and vulnerability probabilities by proposing an approach that considers a TOI and an investment's ability to mitigate the exploitability of that TOI. We then look at the relative importance of the TOI compared with other TOIs based on priority and scope.

## Addressing OPNAV N2/N6 Prioritization Challenges

Our methodology begins to address several of the challenges faced by OPNAV N2/N6, which we discussed in Chapter One, but some challenges will still limit the precision and relevance of the proposed methodology's outputs. For example, the approach is tailored to the limited information available to OPNAV N2/N6. This allows analysts to base their assessments on available data, as opposed to making purely subjective guesses to provide methodology inputs. On the other hand, this tailoring results in methodology outputs that are not informed by threat intelligence and potentially lack an understanding of the baseline (pre-investment) TOI exploitability.

The proposed methodology does allow the comparison of different classes of investments (e.g., system versus process improvements) and scales (e.g., affecting one class of ships versus many). It also derives a cost-effectiveness calculation based on the investment's ability to reduce exploitability. This calculation can be used as a proxy for a relative ROI when comparing investments but does not ultimately quantify the impact (or return) on the potential investment.

Finally, the approach described here provides flexibility for OPNAV N2/N6 to apply several different investment prioritization strategies. Three dimensions of the investment (i.e., cost-effectiveness, impact, and cost of the investment) are provided in a simple comprehensive figure. In our implementation instructions, we provide one way to prioritize investments using these dimensions. However, other strategies can be used based on OPNAV N2/N6 objectives.

In addition to the proposed methodology, we have some ideas about how to address some of the challenges to increase the power of this and other investment prioritization strategies.

## Recommendations

This research gave rise to the following two recommendations beyond the methodology we proposed to help OPNAV and the commands improve the data used for decisionmaking:

1. **Provide a structured data framework for recommended investments, ideally through a web portal instead of PowerPoint slides.** This would, at a minimum, enable OPNAV N2/N6 to compare investments more quickly and mitigate the challenges of comparing past- and future-year investments. The existing FLINT portal could be adapted for this purpose.

2. **Within the data framework, provide common fields that represent DoN priorities and the scope of the investment.** The framework could include additional fields that are useful for econometric analysis. In applying our impact scales, we found that it was challenging to rationalize between investments because we did not know the scope at which they operated (e.g., in terms of numbers of users supported and numbers of ships or aircraft supported or affected). It is critical for investment requests to include this information to increase understanding of a given investment's potential impact relative to others. Similarly, having structured, codified, and consistent priorities across investments enables rapid comparative analysis.

## Next Steps

We are prepared to work with OPNAV N2/N6 to pilot the methodology as part of the upcoming POM process. There are a several ways in which the methodology could be enhanced or adjusted in the future. For example, we could

- incorporate weights on risk factors to allow adjustable user risk perceptions (the current approach is a de facto risk-neutral model)
- incorporate or account for the different types of funding: research and development, procurement, and operations and maintenance
- develop another alternative approach to the ROI-like measure and implement a return-on-attack approach
- incorporate the impact of the investment on the threat attack surface
- develop more examples of how a score could be satisfied (ideally with quantitative measures) over time
- allow investments to vary the impact scales, particularly criticality
- consider the TOI life cycle more broadly (e.g., supply chain, software design, development, delivery, continuous operation).

## Discussion

The private sector struggles with monetizing loss and understanding an organization's vulnerabilities and risks against the backdrop of a myriad of potential attack vectors. However, it is usually possible for the cyber insurance industry to monetize potential losses. DoD cybersecurity investments share many of the same challenges but with the additional challenge that loss is difficult or impossible to quantify monetarily.

Investments in cybersecurity guard against, potentially thwart, or respond to actions by an adversary. However, the investments are more nuanced; for example, they are not necessarily tied to operational scenarios, where the risk of underinvestment can be quantified in terms of failed missions, operational losses, or unmet performance parameters. Cybersecurity risks can be borne out over many years with a wide distribution of consequences, from minor exfiltration of modestly sensitive data to major operational compromise of the Navy's most exquisite systems. Therefore, the benefits of investments in cybersecurity can accrue over a few months or even several years. Furthermore, it is possible that some investments have limited utility, with their primary purpose being to satisfy a legal or regulatory requirement rather than address key DoN priorities. Our methodology is agnostic to the underlying motivation for the investment, but it can still illuminate situations in which investments are not providing value to the fleet.

The evolution of cybersecurity guidelines away from checklist-based approaches and toward goal-oriented outcomes (such as the NIST Risk Management Framework) requires investors to consider the nature of the investment and the role it plays relative to threats; they also must consider whether the results must be represented in decision models. Constructs such as the NIST Cybersecurity Framework provide a way to categorize investments (identify, detect, respond, react, and recover), but the effect of a given investment might be less than straightforward and require broader mission context. For example, it is unclear whether a detection capability should be represented as reducing system vulnerability (the assumption being that detection can lead to interdiction of an attack, thereby stopping it before it is executed) or whether the capability is better represented as affecting loss (the attacker might be successful, but the capability prompts a response and recovery process that minimizes the attack's effects). This is related to but separate from questions regarding the effectiveness of the detection capability itself, which can have a significant impact on the resulting analysis.

Despite the complexity of defining, validating, and analyzing systems, decisionmakers need straightforward metrics against which to judge the value of potential investments in cybersecurity. The limitations and constraints identified in this report constrained the solution space for OPNAV N2/N6 decisions. This, in turn, influenced the design and construction of the methodology presented in Chapter Two, which seeks to overcome (or at least reduce) these constraints in ways that are compatible with the available data and OPNAV N2/N6 needs and timelines.

Although there is certainly room for improvement in the proposed methodology, it is a practical first step toward a more objective and risk-informed approach to prioritizing cyber investments. When compared with existing methods used by OPNAV N2/N6, this methodology should improve the consistency of ratings between analysts and investments and provide a more defined structure for thinking through the risk reduction and prioritization of different investments.

A major advantage of the methodology presented here over others in the security information economic literature is its simplicity. No complex modeling is required. The risk matrixes align with current DoD processes, making the methodology more approachable for analysts. The level of effort required is further reduced by the need to assess only the risk factors that are relevant to an investment.

This simplicity, however, does not compromise the methodology's ability to exercise many important concepts from the mission-centric cybersecurity frameworks highlighted in the beginning of this report. The methodology, for instance, includes concepts from mission thread analysis (e.g., function criticality, fragility) and accounts for the adversary's cost-benefit calculus (e.g., reducing adversary knowledge through continuous cyber maintenance, increasing difficulty of access through complexity of design).

Finally, the proposed methodology is tailored specifically to the information provided and decisions relevant to OPNAV N2/N6 when it needs to make cyber investment priorities. It allows the comparison of different classes of investments, such as systems versus personnel or process improvements; the latter are often overlooked in cybersecurity risk frameworks. It also provides OPNAV N2/N6 decisionmakers with ROI-like measures that are presented with other attributes that mirror relevant objectives, such as mission impact and the total cost of the investment. These three dimensions can be presented for multiple investments in a single figure to facilitate communication and decisionmaking.

APPENDIX

# Relevant Frameworks and Methodologies

This appendix provides further detail on the concepts explored in the development of this research. The information provided is by no means exhaustive, given the expansive literature. Rather, this appendix provides detail that is useful for understanding and contextualizing the research presented in this report.

## Econometrics

Economic metrics (or *econometrics*) involves the employment of business measurements to the problem of investment decisionmaking. As discussed in Chapter One, these metrics form the basis for much of the literature regarding investments in cybersecurity. The common basis for information security economics is the notion of ALE:

$$\text{ALE}_x = p_x \times L,$$

where $L$ is the potential loss and $p_x$ is the probability of incurring that loss within period $x$. For example, if we consider a notional \$1 million loss with a 10-percent chance of being compromised, the calculated ALE would be \$1 million $\times$ 0.10 = \$100,000. Subsequent investments in cybersecurity might seek to reduce ALE by decreasing either the likelihood of the loss (e.g., by making changes that make the system harder to attack or less exposed) or the amount of the potential loss (e.g., by using a cheaper or more segmented system). Assuming that a given cybersecurity investment reduces $p_x$ by some amount, the EBIS enjoyed by that investment is the difference of losses between the current state ($\text{ALE}_0$) and the new state following security investment $s$ ($\text{ALE}_s$):

$$\text{EBIS} = \text{ALE}_0 - \text{ALE}_s = (p_0 \times L) - (p_s \times L).$$

If a security investment reduced the probability of compromise from 10 percent to 5 percent over the period under consideration, the EBIS for that investment would be

$$(\$1 \text{ million} \times 0.10) - (\$1 \text{ million} \times 0.05) = \$50,000.$$

Of course, this is an incomplete picture because it does not consider the cost of the security investment itself. Subtracting the cost of security from the benefit (EBIS) results in the earned net benefit of information security (ENBIS). When divided by the cost of the security, ENBIS yields a measure of the return on security investment (ROSI), or simply ROI:

$$ROSI = ENBIS / s = (ALE_0 - ALE_s - s) / s.$$

If the cost of the investment is \$20,000, then

$$ROSI = ((\$1 \text{ million} \times 0.10) - (\$1 \text{ million} \times 0.05) - \$20,000) / \$20,000,$$

where ROSI = 1.5.

For two investments of \$5,000 and \$20,000, and to reduce the loss likelihood to 8 percent and 6 percent, respectively, we can compute ROSI as follows to determine which is the better investment:

- Investment A ENBIS: (\$1 million × 0.10) – (\$1 million × 0.08) – \$5,000 = \$15,000
- Investment B ENBIS: (\$1 million × 0.10) – (\$1 million × 0.06) – \$20,000 = \$20,000.

In this case, the \$20,000 investment results in a higher return, although both could be considered beneficial investments (because they both have a positive ROSI).

This highlights an important point: Calculations using this approach provide an "optimal" point based on the efficiency of the investment—the best "bang for the buck." In this case, it tracked to the better security outcome (e.g., the lower probability of loss), but this might not always be the case. Had the 6-percent reduction in investment cost \$35,000, the \$5,000 investment would have provided the favorable ROI. Above \$40,000, the return on the 6-percent reduction would have been negative (and, therefore, a "bad" investment).

Given the difficulty in collecting annualized, risk-adjusted security benefit data, some have offered that ROSI and associated metrics "should not be used for anything but negotiating a security budget," advocating instead for the development of more-specific models that employ a two-step process of using security level as an intermediary mapping between costs and benefits (Böhme, 2010, p. 21). This hammers home the point that such ROI- or ROSI-based approaches as the GL model (which we describe later) are far in advance of available data.

## Economic Models

The metrics identified earlier offer a specific view of a particular investment and often lack context or a comparative basis. A growing body of research has resulted in models based on these concepts that support evaluation, insight, and prediction to ultimately support decisionmaking. The literature features numerous investment approaches, employing different underlying theories and mechanisms to target aspects of the information security invest-ment question. However, because of the cross-cutting and emerging nature of the problem, these approaches offer no consensus when it comes to meaningfully defining the boundaries between model categories.

An early review of this literature defined models in terms of decision-theoretic and game-theoretic approaches. The authors make the distinction that game-theoretic models endo-genize effort exerted by the attacker (i.e., the attacker acts strategically, tailoring effort to an assessment of the target's investment level), while decision-theoretic models focus on defender utility (Cavusoglu, Srinivasan, and Yue, 2008, p. 283).

Huang and Behara, 2013, p. 257, further decomposes what the authors refer to as the "base theory" of models in the literature into four categories: economic benefit maximization, risk-based return, game theory, and expected utility theory. However, the work does not define these terms. More recently, Schatz and Bashroush, 2017, examines the pre-2014 literature on investment decisions using a structured review approach. This research identified nine cat-egories, of which utility maximization (UM) and game-theoretic approaches yield the most-novel ideas and are "visibly more influential than other approaches" (Schatz and Bashroush, 2017, pp. 1222–1223). Although the definitions provided for the approach categories are vague and leave room for overlap between them (Schatz and Bashroush, 2017, p. 1216), the catego-ries identified are inclusive of those from prior reviews.

Given this lack of a well-defined ontology for model classification and the prevalence of and relevancy to the DoD/DoN context, we focused on models that employ UM (representa-tive of decision theory) and game theory for the purposes of this research. Approaches can also be combined, forming hybrid models that use both UM and game-theoretic mecha-nisms. Each of these approaches to modeling information security investment was further explored through the literature.

## Utility Maximization

As described in Chapter One, UM models seek to maximize the value obtained by a secu-rity investment without appealing to knowledge of an adversary cost-benefit calculation. The most widely recognized and employed model of this type is the GL model, which was devel-oped in 2002 and originated the stream of one-firm frameworks on cybersecurity investment (Fedele and Roner, 2021).

### Gordon-Loeb Model

In their seminal 2002 paper, Gordon and Loeb derive optimal information security invest-ment for a single risk-neutral firm. It is a single-period decision framework with no endog-enous interaction with other firms, attacker(s), and so on. The most common formulation for GL involves an extension of the base ENBIS calculation, in which an investment ($z$) is related to the security benefit (measured by a reduction of the system vulnerability, $v$) through a function as opposed to a single probability likelihood:

$$\text{ENBIS}(z) = [v - S(z,v)]L - z,$$

where $v$ represents the vulnerability of the system, $L$ represents the potential loss, and $S(z,v)$ is the security breach probability function (SBPF). SBPFs are at the heart of the model, along with assumptions regarding the nature of the investment. In the original GL paper, assumptions of concavity (i.e., all investments contribute positively) and diminishing returns (i.e., increasing investment has less impact) governed the nature of SBPFs; see Figure 1 in Gordon, Loeb, and Zhou, 2016. More formally,

- assumption 1: $\forall\, z, S(z,0) = 0$. If the system is completely vulnerable, no amount of investment leads to change.
- assumption 2: $\forall\, v, S(0,v) = v$. Absent investment, the state of vulnerability is not changed.
- assumption 3: $\forall\, v$ in (0..1) and $\forall\, z \geq 0$, $\partial S(z,v)\,/\,\partial z < 0$, $\partial\partial S\,(z,v)\,/\,\partial\partial z > 0$ and $\lim_{z \to \infty}$ $S(z,v) = 0$. Here, $S(z,v)$ is twice differentiable and convex; that is, with increased $z$, $S$ increases at a decreasing rate so that there are diminishing returns to investment with no ability to achieve perfect security.

Under these three assumptions, Gordon and Loeb defined two SBPFs, identified as $S_{\text{I}}$ and $S_{\text{II}}$.

$$S_{\text{I}}(z,v) = v\,/\,(\alpha z + 1)^{\beta}\ \alpha > 0,\ \beta \geq 1$$

$$S_{\text{II}}(z,v) = v^{(\alpha z + 1)\cdot}\ \alpha > 0.$$

A key but relatively unexplored aspect of the GL investment model is the establishment of appropriate values for the $\alpha$ and $\beta$ parameters for $S_{\text{I}}$ and $S_{\text{II}}$, which represent the effectiveness (i.e., productivity) of the investment. The few published works that provide examples of or explore these variables employ a wide variety of parameters. Some of the most notable values are captured in Table A.1.

As is evident in Table A.1, the values employed for productivity can vary widely (by orders of magnitude), particularly for $\alpha$ in $S_{\text{I}}$. This would support the need to define system-specific SBPFs or parameter values based on the nature of specific investments and security environments; an example of how this was done for software security can be found in Heitzenrater, 2017. Other explorations attempt to relax the original SBPF assumptions to provide alternative conceptualizations, such as a minimal investment before enjoying returns (for example, a hardware purchase). These are described in Hausken, 2006; Willemson, 2006; and Willemson, 2010. The existence of such models is recognized by Gordon and Loeb, 2002, p. 452, with the basis of SBPFs resting on how stated assumptions map to cybersecurity theory and practice.

Key insights from the GL model include the counterintuitive notion that it is not always best to invest more for increasingly vulnerable info sets. Instead, using GL, it can be shown

TABLE A.1

**Utilized Parameters for $S_I$ and $S_{II}$ Security Breach Probability Functions in the Literature**

| Publication | $S_I \, \alpha$ | $S_I \, \beta$ | $S_{II} \, \alpha$ |
|---|---|---|---|
| Gordon and Loeb, 2002 | $0.00001 \, (1.0 \times 10^{-5})$ | 1 | $0.00001 \, (1.0 \times 10^{-5})$ |
| Gordon et al., 2015 | $0.00001 \, (1.0 \times 10^{-5})$ | 1 | N/A |
| Gordon, Loeb, and Zhou, 2016 | 1 | 1–3 | N/A |
| Naldo and Flamini, 2017 | $4.00 \times 10^{-5}$ to $5.02 \times 10^{-5}$ | 1–1.13 | $4.89 \times 10^{-5}$ to $5.12 \times 10^{-5}$ |
| Krutilla et al., 2021[a] | 0.75–1.25 | 1–3 | N/A |
| Gordon, Loeb, and Zhou, 2020 | 0.5 | 1 | N/A |

[a] This paper reformulated SI to support a dynamic model while keeping the same general form.

that it might be best to focus efforts on information sets with a moderate level of inherent vulnerability. This finding depends on the form of breach function, which must be mapped to the expected or demonstrated benefit of an investment. For functional forms employed in Gordon and Loeb, 2002, the authors showed that the firm should spend no more than 37 percent of its expected loss from successful breach under no additional investment:

$$z^* < (1/e)vL.$$

## Gordon-Loeb Model Limitations

Despite its popularity, the GL model remains difficult to apply, with complexity being the most common complaint by those seeking to apply the concept to practical decisions. Even with this complexity, GL makes the following simplifying assumptions to create a streamlined model that is tractable:

- As with all ALE-based models, challenges remain in defining and representing the complex notion of vulnerability as a probability.
- There is an assumption that the information set faces a single threat and that there can be no additional losses because of a second breach (Gordon and Loeb, 2002, pp. 441–442).
- The model does not account for cases in which "a single investment in information security is used to protect the security of multiple information sets having correlated security risks;" it also does not "give guidance on how the total investment in security should be allocated between information security investments and security investments for other assets" (Gordon and Loeb, 2002, p. 452). Both seem to be important considerations for DoN; the latter is especially relevant to PPBE senior decision boards (e.g., Program Review Board, Corporate Board) as they integrate across all resource spon-

sor portfolios, capability domains (e.g., strategic, air, undersea), and program readiness categories (personnel, equipment, supply, training, ordnance, networks, and infrastructure).

- The model also does not account for qualitative aspects of investment decisions—benefits to cybersecurity investments that are not able to be monetized, for example (Gordon, Loeb, and Zhou, 2016, p. 58).
- There is an assumption that SBPFs are smooth functions, when "in reality, discrete investments in new security technologies are often necessary to get any incremental result" (Gordon and Loeb, 2002, p. 442). This is justified through the rationale that "the commitment to invest in security may be made in discrete pieces, [but] the actual expenditures can often be broken down into small increments. Furthermore, some information investments can be reversed (e.g., additional security personnel can be fired and purchased equipment and software can be sold)" (Gordon and Loeb, 2002, p. 442).

Others have echoed and expanded on these concepts. Of note is Böhme, 2010, which explores both philosophical and practical concerns. Analysts often struggle with the level of abstraction in GL analyses, which directly map inputs (monetary amounts of security investment) to outputs (probability of loss) at a high level. In practice, this relationship is difficult to observe. Thus, Böhme advocates for the use of intermediate observable steps, such as security level, that can be captured in more-concrete ways through deterministic (patch level, presence of virus scanners) and stochastic (false alarms, missed detection rates) measures. It is this role that the NIST Cybersecurity Framework plays in the model as presented, but its use creates the challenge of translating security levels into desired actions. This type of mapping speaks more directly to the notion of security productivity and aids in defining the SBPF (Böhme, 2010, pp. 3–4).

Finally, because of their role in model execution, SBPFs and associated parameters must accurately capture the nature of a given investment and target system; this is critical for reliable and employable results. Previous research has examined approaches that consider specific scenarios or types of investments, such as software security (Heitzenrater, 2017) or e-business systems (Tanaka et al., 2005), but these approaches are largely underdeveloped in the literature. According to Gordon and Loeb,

> [t]here is no simple procedure to determine the probabilities of the threat and the vulnerability associated with an information set [or for] deriving and considering the potential loss from an information security breach, especially for a huge loss (as would likely be the case for the protection of many national/public assets). (Gordon and Loeb, 2002, p. 452)[1]

---

[1] The authors explain that their model "is not intended to cover protection of national/public assets or other circumstances where a loss could be catastrophic," insofar as such a loss would render their risk-neutrality assumption unrealistic (p. 441). This further limits the model's applicability to a DoD operating environment.

To date, it appears that no studies have adapted these concepts to other risk positions in research and development or the sustainment context—military or otherwise.

## Gordon-Loeb Model Extensions

From the basis established by GL, many variations and extensions have been proposed to address these concerns. We note a few here that are relevant to the proposed framework.

Wang, 2019, attempts to distinguish between different types of cybersecurity investment by introducing categories of investment and optimizing the mix between them. This method uses average spending data and mitigation cost-benefit information to calculate "effectiveness indices" for investments (Wang, 2019, p. 8). Although this approach compounds the challenge of employing GL, the investment categorization method spans the exploitability dimensions employed in our proposed framework.

Others have examined the assumption of data set independence, developing models that examine interdependency and spillover between information sets. Fedele and Roner, 2021, builds on the GL model to guide firms' investments when they operate a common network. Although the problem of "technical spillover" is of interest to DoN, this model extension introduces a host of unrealistic assumptions: in addition to risk-neutrality (discussed earlier) and the consideration of strictly additive impacts, the model assumes that the information sets in question are symmetric and that network topology is *exogenously* determined. Finally, the SBPF requires the specification of a coefficient that captures the relative effectiveness of investments for each information set existing on the shared network.

## Game Theoretic Models

A second class of models involves the application of game theory to the problem of cybersecurity investment decisionmaking. These models use a strategic, mathematical approach that displays the utility for both attackers and defenders (Schatz and Bashroush, 2017). In doing so, these models address deficiencies identified by such researchers as Cavusoglu, Srinivasan, and Yue, 2008, who contend that "[t]he reason for the limitation of traditional models, when applied to analyze IT security problems, can be stated as one simple proposition: *They do not allow a firm's security investment to influence the behavior of hackers*" (Cavusoglu, Srinivasan, and Yue, 2008, p. 283; emphasis in original).

Varian, 2004, defines multiple game constructs to describe various information security investment concepts, as follows:

- weakest link, in which the attacker has a single success against a system with multiple end points (the weakest link in the system)
- total effort, in which the attacker's success depends on the total effort across all end points
- best shot, in which the attacker's success is predicated on the best effort against any single end point.

Others have introduced additional models, as well as variations on those described here, to capture key aspects of defender and attacker interactions (for example, Grossklags, Christin, and Chuang, 2008). However, with little information regarding expected attacker behavior or utility, these approaches were deemed unlikely to meet OPNAV N2/N6's needs.

## Hybrid Models

A final class combines the other two modeling approaches to derive the positive aspects of each. Such hybrid approaches seek to employ measurable utility-based metrics within an adversary-driven framework. In doing so, they often codify or abstract specific attacker behavior, employing utility-maximization in place of equilibrium identification.

This style of model is perhaps best exemplified by the IWL model introduced in Böhme and Moore, 2016, and discussed in Chapter One. IWL incorporates several parameters, which are summarized in Table A.1 in Böhme and Moore, 2016. These parameters include asset value, time (number of periods), and rate of return per period; for the attacker, the projected number of threats, amount of loss (as a percentage of asset value), minimum and subsequent attack costs, and level of uncertainty; and for defense, the individual and sunk costs for defense and interdependence.

Game-theoretic metrics, such as attacker gain, and such conceptual parameters as uncertainty further add to the complexity of employing hybrid models (such as IWL) to the Navy cyber investment problem. These challenges are further explored using OPNAV N2/N6 data in a separate appendix that is not available to the general public.

## Conclusions

This discussion represents only a segment of a large and growing body of literature around the problem of information security investment decision support. The research highlighted here is intended to provide insight into key concepts and principles introduced elsewhere in this research.

Although the overall finding is that the limited data available to OPNAV N2/N6 undermine the ability to use the majority of models in the literature, examining them is informative to Navy investment goals. The power of ROSI, GL, IWL, and similar models is not in their direct application but instead in their ability to focus attention on specific aspects of investment questions that might otherwise be overlooked. Therefore, these models may find the most utility in their potential to generate unique, general insights and identify characteristics and/or mechanisms that can be incorporated in bespoke models, such as the model developed and discussed in Chapter Two.

One area where DoD investments differ from those in the private sector is that there is no ability to fund additional projects through raising capital. Most firms have some flexibility to engage in investments that meet a cost of capital requirement. In DoD, funding is typically fixed and "zero-sum," so alternatives must compete for funding; thus, a limited subset of alternatives can be implemented. Therefore, approaches that use investment returns or offer open-ended results for ideal investment levels will have limited applicability if the results exceed budgeted thresholds.

Related to this issue is the siloed nature of DoD funds, which limits the use of budgets based on the type and scope of investment. DoD invests in cybersecurity in different ways, including by making research and development investments into improved (or novel) capability, deploying capabilities that address a specific concern, and managing the operations and sustainment funding that maintains that capability. In the context of investment modeling that seeks to minimize complexity, the interdependent relationship between funding streams and their subsequent impact on various model parameters (including vulnerability, effectiveness, and potential loss) is difficult to capture thoroughly and succinctly.

Perhaps the most critical takeaway from this review is that model-based analysis is predicated on notions of optimization (in the case of UM) and equilibrium (in the game-theoretic case). Neither of these is necessarily the "best" outcome or "winning" situation, but these notions yield a result that balances cost and benefit in a risk-neutral scenario. In short, economic optimality is not the same as "most secure."

To overcome the limitations of modeling approaches, the lack of a clear leading modeling approach, and the challenge of optimality, these concepts must be adapted to the DoD context to provide practicality to their employment. As a result, we leveraged past RAND research in cybersecurity life cycle management (Snyder et al., 2015) and cybersecurity measurement (Snyder et al., 2020) to inform the development of the model framework presented in Chapter Two. Overcoming the identified limitations and further unifying DoD-specific approaches with the theory and concepts presented in the broader literature is a rich source of potential future research.

# Abbreviations

| | |
|---|---|
| ALE | annualized loss expectancy |
| CANES | Consolidated Afloat Networks and Enterprise Services |
| CNO | chief of naval operations |
| CRA | Cyber Risk Assessment |
| CVAST | Cyber Vulnerability Assessment Tool |
| CVN | nuclear aircraft carrier |
| DDG | guided missile destroyer |
| DoD | U.S Department of Defense |
| DoN | U.S. Department of the Navy |
| EBIS | earned benefit of information security |
| ENBIS | earned net benefit of information security |
| ERE | exploitability reduction effectiveness |
| FLINT | Force Level Integration Tool |
| FY | fiscal year |
| FYDP | Future Years Defense Program |
| GL | Gordon-Loeb |
| HM&E | hull, mechanical, and electrical |
| IT | information technology |
| IWL | iterated weakest link |
| LPD | landing platform dock |
| NAVAIR | Naval Air Systems Command |
| NAVSEA | Naval Sea Systems Command |
| NAVWAR | Naval Information Warfare Systems Command |
| NIST | National Institute of Standards and Technology |
| OPNAV | Office of the Chief of Naval Operations |
| OPNAV N2/N6 | Office of the Chief of Naval Operations for Information Warfare |
| POM | program objective memorandum |
| PPBE | Planning, Programming, Budgeting, and Execution |
| ROI | return on investment |
| ROSI | return on security investment |
| SBPF | security breach probability function |
| SWAN | Shipboard Wide Area Network |
| TOI | target of investment |
| UM | utility maximization |

# References

Anderson, Ross, "Why Information Security is Hard—An Economic Perspective," *Proceedings of the 17th Annual Computer Security Applications Conference*, Washington, D.C.: IEEE, 2001, pp. 358–365.

Blickstein, Irv, John Yurchak, Bradley Martin, Jerry M. Sollinger, and Daniel Tremblay, *Navy Planning, Programming, Budgeting, and Execution: A Reference Guide for Senior Leaders, Managers, and Action Officers*, Santa Monica, Calif.: RAND Corporation, TL-224-NAVY, 2016. As of December 13, 2021:
https://www.rand.org/pubs/tools/TL224.html

Böhme, Rainer, "Security Metrics and Security Investment Models," in Isao Echizen, Noboru Kunihiro, and Ryoichi Sasaki, eds., *Advances in Information and Computer Security*, Berlin, Germany: Springer, 2010, pp. 10–24.

Böhme, Rainer, and Tyler Moore, *Security Metrics and Security Investment*, Dallas, Tex.: Southern Methodist University, working paper, September 9, 2013.

———, "The 'Iterated Weakest Link' Model of Adaptive Security Investment," *Journal of Information Security*, Vol. 7, No. 2, 2016.

Burke, David A., and Edward R. Morgan, "NAVAIR Cyber Risk Assessment," briefing presented at Project Management Institute, Southern Maryland Chapter, Naval Air Station Patuxent River, Md., June 19, 2018. As of December 13, 2021:
https://pmisomd.org/events/presentations/609-20180619-cwd-cra-briefing/file

Cancian, Mark F., *U.S. Military Forces in FY 2020: SOF, Civilians, Contractors, and Nukes*, Washington, D.C.: Center for Strategic and International Studies, October 2019.

Cavusoglu, Huseyin, Raghunathan Srinivasan, and Wei T. Yue, "Decision-Theoretic and Game-Theoretic Approaches to IT Security Investment," *Journal of Management Information Systems*, Vol. 25, No. 2, 2008, pp. 281–304.

Cremonini, Marco, and Patrizia Martini, "Evaluating Information Security Investments from Attackers' Perspective: The Return-on-Attack (ROA)," paper presented at the Workshop on the Economics of Information Security, Harvard University, Cambridge, Mass., 2005.

DoD Instruction—*See* U.S. Department of Defense Instruction.

DoN—*See* U.S. Department of the Navy.

Executive Order 13800, "Strengthening the Cybersecurity of Federal Networks and Critical Infrastructure," *Federal Register*, Vol. 82, No. 93, May 11, 2017, pp. 22391–22397.

Fedele, Alessandro, and Cristian Roner, "Dangerous Games: A Literature Review on Cybersecurity Investments," *Journal of Economic Surveys*, Vol. 36, No. 1, July 26, 2021, pp. 157–187.

GBS Group, "GBS Awarded $12.6M Code 531 NSWCPD Contract," webpage, undated. As of December 13, 2021:
https://www.thegbsgroup.us/case_study/federal-531-article-naval-contract

Gilligan, John, *The Economics of Cybersecurity: A Practical Framework for Cybersecurity Investment*, Fair Lakes, Va.: AFCEA International Cyber Committee, Economics of Cybersecurity Subcommittee, October 2013.

Gordon, Lawrence A., and Martin P. Loeb, "The Economics of Information Security Investment," *ACM Transactions on Information and System Security*, Vol. 5, No. 4, November 2002, pp. 438–457.

Gordon, Lawrence A., Martin P. Loeb, William Lucyshyn, and Lei Zhou, "The Impact of Information Sharing on Cybersecurity Underinvestment: A Real Options Perspective," *Journal of Accounting and Public Policy*, Vol. 34, No. 5, September–October 2015, pp. 509–519.

Gordon, Lawrence A., Martin P. Loeb, and Lei Zhou, "Investing in Cybersecurity: Insights from the Gordon-Loeb Model," *Journal of Information Security*, Vol. 7, No. 2, March 2016, pp. 49–59.

———, "Integrating Cost-Benefit Analysis into the NIST Cybersecurity Framework via the Gordon–Loeb Model," *Journal of Cybersecurity*, Vol. 6, No. 1, 2020.

Grossklags, Jens, Nicolas Christin, and John Chuang, "Secure or Insecure? A Game-Theoretic Analysis of Information Security Games," *Proceedings of the 17th International Conference on the World Wide Web*, Beijing, China, April 21–25, 2008, New York: Association for Computing Machinery, April 2018, pp. 209–218.

Heitzenrater, Chad D., *Software Security Investment Modelling for Decision-Support*, dissertation, Oxford, UK: University of Oxford, 2017.

Hausken, Kjell, "Returns to Information Security Investment: The Effect of Alternative Information Security Breach Functions on Optimal Investment and Sensitivity to Vulnerability," *Information Systems Frontiers*, Vol. 8, No. 5, January 2006, pp. 338–349.

Huang, C. Derrick, and Ravi S. Behara, "Economics of Information Security Investment in the Case of Concurrent Heterogeneous Attacks with Budget Constraints," *International Journal of Production Economics*, Vol. 141, No. 1, January 2013, pp. 255–268.

Kern, Steven B., "Naval Aviation Weapon System Cyber Risk Assessment Methodologies," briefing presented at the NATO Systems Concepts and Integration Specialists Meeting, Fort Walton Beach, Fla., May 8, 2018. As of December 13, 2021: https://www.sto.nato.int/publications/STO%20Meeting%20Proceedings/STO-MP-SCI-300/MP-SCI-300-12P.pdf

Krutilla, Kerry, Alexander Alexeev, Eric Jardine, and David Good, "The Benefits and Costs of Cybersecurity Risk Reduction: A Dynamic Extension of the Gordon and Loeb Model," *Risk Analysis*, Vol. 41, No. 10, October 2021, pp. 1795–1808.

McDermot, Kara, "NAVWAR Develops 'Cybersecurity Scorecard' to Facilitate Data-Driven Decisions," U.S. Navy, October 9, 2019. As of December 13, 2021: https://www.navy.mil/Press-Office/News-Stories/Article/2239877/navwar-develops-cybersecurity-scorecard-to-facilitate-data-driven-decisions

Naldo, Maurizio, and Marta Flamini, "Calibration of the Gordon-Loeb Models for the Probability of Security Breaches," *Proceedings of the UKSim-AMSS 19th International Conference on Modelling & Simulation, Cambridge*, United Kingdom, 5–7 April 2017, Piscataway, N.J.: IEEE, 2017, pp. 135–140.

NAVAIR—*See* Naval Air Systems Command.

Naval Air Systems Command, *NAVAIR Cyber Risk Assessment (CRA) Methodology: Implementation Guide*, SWP-4000-001, Version R8-1, February 13, 2019.

National Institute of Standards and Technology, *Guide for Conducting Risk Assessments*, Gaithersburg, Md., NIST Special Publication 800-30, rev. 1, September 2012.

———, *Framework for Improving Critical Infrastructure Cybersecurity*, Gaithersburg, Md., version 1.1, April 16, 2018.

Newman, Lily Hay, "The Clever 'Double Agent' Attack Turns Antivirus into Malware," *Wired*, March 23, 2017. As of December 2, 2021:
https://www.wired.com/2017/03/clever-doubleagent-attack-turns-antivirus-malware

Nieles, Michael, Kelley L. Dempsey, and Victoria Yan Pillitteri, *An Introduction to Information Security*, Gaithersburg, Md.: National Institute of Standards and Technology, NIST Special Publication 800-12, rev. 1, June 2017.

NIST—*See* National Institute of Standards and Technology.

Program Executive Office for Manpower, Logistics, and Business Solutions, "Enterprise Systems & Services & Innovation Support Services," fact sheet, Naval Information Warfare Systems Command, May 2021.

Public Law 113-283, Federal Information Security Modernization Act of 2014, December 18, 2014.

Romanosky, Sasha, Lillian Ablon, Andreas Kuehn, and Therese Jones, "Content Analysis of Cyber Insurance Policies: How Do Carriers Price Cyber Risk?" *Journal of Cybersecurity*, Vol. 5, No. 1, 2019.

Ross, Ron, Michael McEvilley, and Janet Carrier Oren, *Systems Security Engineering: Considerations for a Multidisciplinary Approach in the Engineering of Trustworthy Secure Systems*, Gaithersburg, Md.: National Institute of Standards and Technology, NIST Special Publication 800-160, March 21, 2018.

Schatz, Daniel, and Rabih Bashroush, "Economic Valuation for Information Security Investment: A Systematic Literature Review," *Information Systems Frontiers*, Vol. 19, 2017, pp. 1205–1228.

Schechter, Stuart, "Quantitatively Differentiating System Security," paper presented at Workshop on the Economics of Information Security, University of California, Berkeley, May 17, 2002.

Sndyer, Don, Elizabeth Bodine-Baron, Dahlia Anne Goldfeld, Bernard Fox, Myron Hura, Mahyar A. Amouzegar, and Lauren Kendrick, *Cyber Mission Thread Analysis: A Prototype Framework for Assessing Impact to Missions from Cyber Attacks to Weapon Systems*, Santa Monica, Calif.: RAND Corporation, RR-3188/1-AF, 2022. As of May 15, 2022:
https://www.rand.org/pubs/research_reports/RR3188z1.html

Snyder, Don, Lauren A. Mayer, Guy Weichenberg, Danielle C. Tarraf, Bernard Fox, Myron Hura, Suzanne Genc, and Jonathan William Welburn, *Measuring Cybersecurity and Cyber Resiliency*, Santa Monica, Calif.: RAND Corporation, RR-2703-AF, 2020. As of December 13, 2021:
https://www.rand.org/pubs/research_reports/RR2703.html

Snyder, Don, James D. Powers, Elizabeth Bodine-Baron, Bernard Fox, Lauren Kendrick, and Michael H. Powell, *Improving the Cybersecurity of U.S. Air Force Military Systems Throughout Their Life Cycles*, Santa Monica, Calif.: RAND Corporation, RR-1007-AF, 2015. As of December 13, 2021:
http://www.rand.org/pubs/research_reports/RR1007.html

Tanaka, Hideyuki, Kanta Matsuura, and Osamu Sudoh, "Vulnerability and Information Security Investment: An Empirical Analysis of e-local Government in Japan," *Journal of Accounting and Public Policy*, Vol. 24, No. 1, January–February 2005, pp. 37–59.

U.S. Department of Defense Chief Information Officer, *Cybersecurity Strategy Outline and Guidance*, version 1.4, Washington, D.C., June 24, 2021.

U.S. Department of Defense Instruction 8510.01, *Risk Management Framework (RMF) for DoD Information Technology (IT)*, Washington, D.C., December 29, 2020.

U.S. Department of Defense Instruction 5000.90, *Cybersecurity for Acquisition Decision Authorities and Program Managers*, Washington, D.C., December 31, 2020.

U.S. Department of Homeland Security, *DHS Risk Lexicon: 2010 Edition*, Washington, D.C., September 2010.

U.S. Department of the Navy, *Department of Defense Fiscal Year (FY) 2018 Budget Estimates: Justification Book,* Volume 1 of 5, *Other Procurement, Navy, BA 1*, Washington, D.C., May 2017a. As of December 13, 2021:
https://www.secnav.navy.mil/fmc/fmb/Documents/18pres/OPN_BA1_BOOK.pdf

———, *Department of Defense Fiscal Year (FY) 2018 Budget Estimates: Justification Book,* Volume 2 of 5, *Other Procurement, Navy, BA 2*, Washington, D.C., May 2017b. As of December 13, 2021:
https://www.secnav.navy.mil/fmc/fmb/Documents/18pres/OPN_BA2_BOOK.pdf

———, *Department of Defense Fiscal Year (FY) 2018 Budget Estimates: Justification Book,* Volume 2 of 5, *Research, Development, Testing, and Evaluation, Navy, Budget Activity 4*, Washington, D.C., May 2017c. As of December 13, 2021:
https://www.secnav.navy.mil/fmc/fmb/Documents/18pres/RDTEN_BA4_Book.pdf

———, *Department of Defense Fiscal Year (FY) 2018 Budget Estimates: Justification Book,* Volume 5 of 5, *Other Procurement, Navy, BA 5–8*, Washington, D.C., May 2017d. As of December 13, 2021:
https://www.secnav.navy.mil/fmc/fmb/Documents/18pres/OPN_BA_5-8_Book.pdf

———, *Department of Defense Fiscal Year (FY) 2020 Budget Estimates: Justification Book, Volume 1 of 5, Other Procurement, Navy, BA 0–1*, Washington, D.C., March 2019a. As of May 24, 2022:
https://www.secnav.navy.mil/fmc/fmb/Documents/20pres/OPN_BA1_BOOK.pdf

———, *Department of Defense Fiscal Year (FY) 2020 Budget Estimates: Justification Book, Volume 3 of 5, Research, Development, Test & Evaluation, Navy, Budget Activity 5*, Washington, D.C., March 2019b. As of May 24, 2022:
https://www.secnav.navy.mil/fmc/fmb/Documents/20pres/RDTEN_BA5_Book.pdf

———, *Department of Defense Fiscal Year (FY) 2020 Budget Estimates: Justification Book,* Volume 4 of 5, *Research, Development, Test & Evaluation, Navy, Budget Activity 6*, Washington, D.C., March 2019c. As of May 24, 2022:
https://www.secnav.navy.mil/fmc/fmb/Documents/20pres/RDTEN_BA6_book.pdf

———, *CNO NAVPLAN*, Washington, D.C., January 2021.

U.S. Department of the Navy, Deputy Assistant Secretary of the Navy (Budget), *Highlights of the Department of the Navy FY 2021 Budget*, Washington, D.C., February 10, 2020.

U.S. Government Accountability Office, "SolarWinds Cyberattack Demands Significant Federal and Private-Sector Response," blog, April 22, 2021. As of December 2, 2021:
https://www.gao.gov/blog/solarwinds-cyberattack-demands-significant-federal-and-private-sector-response-infographic

Varian, Hal R., "How to Build an Economic Model in Your Spare Time," *American Economist*, Vol. 61, No. 1, 1997, pp. 81–90.

———, "System Reliability and Free Riding," *Economics of Information Security*, 2004, pp. 1-16.

Wang, Shaun S., "Integrated Framework for Information Security Investment and Cyber Insurance," *Pacific-Basin Finance Journal*, Vol. 57, October 2019, article 101173.

Weis, Aaron D., Chief Information Officer, U.S. Department of the Navy, and Frederick J. Stefany, Acting Assistant Secretary of the Navy for Research, Development, and Acquisition, "Strategic Intent for Transition to Naval Enterprise Information Technology Services," memorandum, October, 7, 2021.

Willemson, Jan, "On the Gordon & Loeb Model for Information Security Investment," paper presented at the Workshop on the Economics of Information Security, University of Cambridge, June 26, 2006.

———, "Extending the Gordon & Loeb Model for Information Security Investment," *Proceedings of the Fifth International Conference on Availability, Reliability, and Security*, Krakow, Poland, 15–18 February 2010, Los Alamitos, Calif.: IEEE, 2010, pp. 258–261.

Xue, Feng, "Attacking Antivirus," *Black Hat Europe*, 2008.